BRIGHT NOTES

THE TEMPEST BY WILLIAM SHAKESPEARE

Intelligent Education

Nashville, Tennessee

BRIGHT NOTES: The Tempest
www.BrightNotes.com

No part of this publication may be used or reproduced in any manner whatsoever without written permission, except in the case of brief quotations in critical articles and reviews. For permissions, contact Influence Publishers http://www.influencepublishers.com.

ISBN: 978-1-645425-88-5 (Paperback)
ISBN: 978-1-645425-89-2 (eBook)

Published in accordance with the U.S. Copyright Office Orphan Works and Mass Digitization report of the register of copyrights, June 2015.

Originally published by Monarch Press.
Ralph A. Ranald, 1964
2020 Edition published by Influence Publishers.

Interior design by Lapiz Digital Services. Cover Design by Thinkpen Designs.

Printed in the United States of America.

Library of Congress Cataloging-in-Publication Data forthcoming.
Names: Intelligent Education
Title: BRIGHT NOTES: The Tempest
Subject: STU004000 STUDY AIDS / Book Notes

CONTENTS

1) Introduction to William Shakespeare — 1

2) Introduction to The Tempest — 12

3) Textual Analysis — 18
    Act I — 18
    Act II — 41
    Act III — 61
    Act IV — 82
    Act V — 95

4) Character Analyses — 106

5) Criticism — 117

6) Bibliography — 136

INTRODUCTION TO WILLIAM SHAKESPEARE

FACTS VERSUS SPECULATION

Anyone who wishes to know where documented truth ends and where speculation begins in Shakespearean scholarship and criticism first needs to know the facts of Shakespeare's life. A medley of life records suggest, by their lack of inwardness, how little is known of Shakespeare's ideology, his beliefs and opinions.

William Shakespeare was baptized on April 26, 1564, as "Gulielmus filius Johannes Shakspere"; the evidence is the parish register of Holy Trinity Church, Stratford, England.

HUSBAND AND FATHER

On November 28, 1582, the Bishop of Worcester issued a license to William Shakespeare and "Anne Hathaway of Stratford" to solemnize a marriage upon one asking of the banns providing that there were no legal impediments. Three askings of the banns were (and are) usual in the Church of England.

On May 26, 1583, the records of the parish church in Stratford note the baptism of Susanna, daughter to William Shakespeare. The inference is clear, then, that Anne Hathaway Shakespeare was with child at the time of her wedding.

On February 2, 1585, the records of the parish church in Stratford note the baptisms of "Hamnet & Judeth, sonne and daughter to William Shakspere."

SHAKESPEARE INSULTED

On September 20, 1592, Robert Greene's A Groats-worth of witte, bought with a million of Repentance was entered in the Stationers' Register. In this work Shakespeare was publicly insulted as "an upstart Crow, beautified with our ["gentlemen" playwrights usually identified as Marlowe, Nashe, and Lodge] feathers, that with Tygers hart wrapt in a Players hyde [a **parody** of a Shakespearean line in II *Henry VI*] supposes he is as well able to bombast out a **blank verse** as the best of you: and being an absolute Iohannes fac totum, is in his own conceit the only Shake-scene in a country." This statement asperses not only Shakespeare's art but intimates his base, i.e., non-gentle, birth. A "John factotum" is a servant or a man of all work.

On April 18, 1593, Shakespeare's long erotic poem *Venus and Adonis* was entered for publication. It was printed under the author's name and was dedicated to the nineteen-year-old Henry Wriothesley, Earl of Southampton.

On May 9, 1594, another long erotic poem, *The Rape of Lucrece*, was entered for publication. It also was printed under Shakespeare's name and was dedicated to the Earl of Southampton.

On December 26 and 27, 1594, payment was made to Shakespeare and others for performances at court by the Lord Chamberlain's servants.

For August 11, 1596, the parish register of Holy Trinity Church records the burial of "Hamnet filius William Shakspere."

FROM "VILLEIN" TO "GENTLEMAN"

On October 20, 1596, John Shakespeare, the poet's father, was made a "gentleman" by being granted the privilege of bearing a coat of arms. Thus, William Shakespeare on this day also became a "gentleman." Shakespeare's mother, Mary Arden Shakespeare, was "gentle" by birth. The poet was a product of a cross-class marriage. Both the father and the son were technically "villeins" or "villains" until this day.

On May 24, 1597, William Shakespeare purchased New Place, a large house in the center of Stratford.

CITED AS "BEST"

In 1598 Francis Meres's *Palladis Tamia* listed Shakespeare more frequently than any other English author. Shakespeare was cited as one of eight by whom "the English tongue is mightily enriched, and gorgeouslie invested in rare ornaments and resplendent abiliments"; as one of six who had raised monumentum aere perennius [a monument more lasting than brass]; as one of five who excelled in lyric poetry; as one of thirteen "best for Tragedie," and as one of seventeen who were "best for Comedy."

On September 20, 1598, Shakespeare is said on the authority of Ben Jonson (in his collection of plays, 1616) to have been an actor in Jonson's *Every Man in His Humour*.

On September 8, 1601, the parish register of Holy Trinity in Stratford records the burial of "Mr. Johannes Shakespeare," the poet's father.

BECOMES A "KING'S MAN"

In 1603 Shakespeare was named among others, the Lord Chamberlain's players, as licensed by James I (Queen Elizabeth having died) to become the King's Men.

In 1603 a garbled and pirated *Hamlet* (now known as *Q1*) was printed with Shakespeare's name on the title page.

In March 1604, King James gave Shakespeare, as one of the Grooms of the Chamber (by virtue of being one of the King's Men), four yards of red cloth for a livery, this being in connection with a royal progress through the City of London.

In 1604 (probably) there appeared a second version of *Hamlet* (now known as *Q2*), enlarged and corrected, with Shakespeare's name on the title page.

On June 5, 1607, the parish register at Stratford records the marriage of "M. John Hall gentleman & Susanna Shaxspere," the poet's elder daughter. John Hall was a doctor of medicine.

BECOMES A GRANDFATHER

On February 21, 1608, the parish register at Holy Trinity, Stratford, records the baptism of Elizabeth Hall, Shakespeare's first grandchild.

On September 9, 1608, the parish register at Holy Trinity, Stratford, records the burial of Mary Shakespeare, the poet's mother.

On May 20, 1609, "Shakespeares Sonnets. Never before Imprinted" was entered for publication.

On February 10, 1616, the marriage of Judith, Shakespeare's younger daughter, is recorded in the parish register of Holy Trinity, Stratford.

On March 25, 1616, Shakespeare made his will. It is extant.

On April 23, 1616, Shakespeare died. The monument in the Stratford church is authority for the date.

BURIED IN STRATFORD CHURCH

On April 25, 1616, Shakespeare was buried in Holy Trinity Church, Stratford. Evidence of this date is found in the church register. A stone laid over his grave bears the inscription:

Good Frend for Jesus Sake Forbeare, To Digg The Dust Encloased Heare! Blest Be Ye Man Yt Spares Thes Stones, And Curst Be He Yt Moves My Bones.

DEMAND FOR MORE INFORMATION

These are the life records of Shakespeare. Biographers, intent on book length or even short accounts of the life of the poet, of necessity flesh out these (and other) not very revealing notices from 1564-1616, Shakespeare's life span with ancillary matter such as the status of Elizabethan actors, details of the Elizabethan theaters, and life under Elizabeth I and James I. Information about Shakespeare's artistic life-for example, his alteration of his sources-is much more abundant than truthful insights into his personal life, including his beliefs. There is, of course, great demand for colorful stories about Shakespeare, and there is intense pressure on biographers to depict the poet as a paragon of wisdom.

ANECDOTES-TRUE OR UNTRUE?

Biographers of Shakespeare may include stories about Shakespeare that have been circulating since at least the seventeenth century; no one knows whether or not these stories are true. One declares that Shakespeare was an apprentice to a butcher, that he ran away from his master, and was received by actors in London. Another story holds that Shakespeare was, in his youth, a schoolmaster somewhere in the country. Another story has Shakespeare fleeing from his native town to escape the clutches of Sir Thomas Lucy who had often had him whipped and sometimes imprisoned for poaching deer. Yet another story represents the youthful Shakespeare as holding horses and taking care of them while their owners attended the theater. And there are other stories.

Scholarly and certainly lay expectations oblige Shakespearean biographers often to resort to speculation. This may be very well if biographers use such words as conjecture, presumably, seems, and almost certainly. I quote an example of this kind of hedged thought and language from Hazelton Spencer's *The Art and Life of William Shakespeare* (1940); "Of politics Shakespeare seems to have steered clear ... but at least by implication Shakespeare reportedly endorses the strong-monarchy policy of the Tudors and Stuarts." Or one may say, as I do in my book *Blood Will Tell in Shakespeare's Plays* (1984): "Shakespeare particularly faults his numerous villeins for lacking the classical virtue of courage (they are cowards) and for deficiencies in reasoning ability (they are 'fools'), and in speech (they commit malapropisms), for lack of charity, for ambition, for unsightly faces and poor physiques, for their smell, and for their harboring lice." This remark is not necessarily biographical or reflective of Shakespeare's personal beliefs; it refers to Shakespeare's art in that it makes general assertions about the base - those who lacked coats of arms-as they appear in the poet's thirty-seven plays. The remark's truth or lack of truth may be tested by examination of Shakespeare's writings.

WHO WROTE SHAKESPEARE'S PLAYS?

The less reputable biographers of Shakespeare, including some of weighty names, state assumptions as if they were facts concerning the poet's beliefs. Perhaps the most egregious are those who cannot conceive that the Shakespearean plays were written by a person not a graduate of Oxford or Cambridge and destitute of the insights permitted by foreign travel and by life at court. Those of this persuasion insist that the seventeenth Earl of Oxford, Edward de Vere (whose descendant Charles Vere recently spoke up for the Earl's authorship of the Shakespearean plays), or Sir Francis Bacon, or someone else wrote the Shakespearean plays. It is also argued that the stigma of publication would besmirch the honor of an Elizabethan gentleman who published under his own name (unless he could pretend to correct a pirated printing of his writings).

BEN JONSON KNEW HIM WELL

Suffice it here to say that the thought of anyone writing the plays and giving them to the world in the name of Shakespeare would have astonished Ben Jonson, a friend of the poet, who literally praised Shakespeare to the skies for his comedies and tragedies in the fine poem "To the Memory of My Beloved Master the Author, Mr. William Shakespeare, and What He Hath Left Us" (printed in the *First Folio*, 1623). Much more commonplace and therefore much more obtrusive upon the minds of Shakespeare students are those many scholars who are capable of writing, for example, that Shakespeare put more of himself into *Hamlet* than any of his other characters or that the poet had no rigid system of religion or morality. Even George Lyman Kittredge, the greatest American Shakespearean, wrote, "Hamlet's advice to the players has always been understood - and rightly - to embody Shakespeare's own views on the art of acting."

In point of fact, we know nothing of Shakespeare's beliefs or opinions except such obvious inferences as that he must have thought New Place, Stratford, worth buying because he bought it. Even Homer, a very self-effacing poet, differs in this matter from Shakespeare. Twice in the *Iliad* he speaks in his own voice (distinguished from the dialogue of his characters) about certain evil deeds of Achilles. Shakespeare left no letters, no diary, and no prefaces (not counting conventionally obsequious dedications); no Elizabethan Boswell tagged Shakespeare around London and the provinces to record his conversation and thus to reveal his mind. In his plays Shakespeare employed no rainsonneur, or authorial mouthpiece, as some other dramatists have done: contrary to many scholarly assertions, it cannot be proved that Prospero, in *The Tempest* in the speech ending "I'll drown my book" (Act V), and Ulysses, in *Troilus and Cressida* in the long speech on "degree" (Act II), speak Shakespeare's own sentiments. All characters in all Shakespearean plays speak for themselves. Whether they speak also for Shakespeare cannot be proved because documents outside the plays cannot be produced.

As for the sonnets, they have long been the happy hunting ground of biographical crackpots who lack outside documents, who do not recognize that Shakespeare may have been using a persona, and who seem not to know that in Shakespeare's time good **sonnets** were supposed to read like confessions.

Some critics even go to the length of professing to hear Shakespeare speaking in the speech of a character and uttering his private beliefs. An example may be found in A. L. Rowse's *What Shakespeare Read and Thought* (1981): "Nor is it so difficult to know what Shakespeare thought or felt. A writer, Logan Pearsall Smith, had the perception to see that a personal tone of voice enters when Shakespeare is telling you what he thinks, sometimes almost a raised voice; it is more obvious again when he urges the same point over and over."

BUT THERE'S NO PROOF!

Rowse, deeply enamoured of his ability to hear Shakespeare's own thoughts in the speeches of characters speaking in character, published a volume entitled Shakespeare's *Self-Portrait, Passages from His Work* (1984). One critic might hear Shakespeare voicing his own thoughts in a speech in *Hamlet*; another might hear the author in *Macbeth*. Shakespearean writings can become a vast whispering gallery where Shakespeare himself is heard hic et ubique (here and everywhere), without an atom of documentary proof.

"BETTER SO"

Closer to truth is Matthew Arnold's poem on Shakespeare:

> Others abide our question. Thou art free. We ask and ask - thou smilest and art still, Out-topping knowledge. For the loftiest hill, Who to the stars uncrowns his majesty, Planting his steadfast footsteps in the sea, Making the heaven of heavens his dwelling Spares but the cloudy border of his base To the foiled searching of mortality; And thou, who didst the stars and sunbeams know, Self-schooled, self-scanned, self-honored, self-secure, Didst tread the earth unguessed at. - Better so....

Here Arnold has Dichtung und Wahrheit - both poetry and truth - with at least two abatements: he exaggerates Shakespeare's wisdom - the poet, after all, is not God; and Arnold fails to acknowledge that Shakespeare's genius was variously recognized in his own time. Jonson, for example, recorded that the "players [actors of the poet's time] have often mentioned it as an honor to Shakespeare, that in his writing (whatsoever he penned) he never blotted a line" (*Timber*), and of course there is praise of Shakespeare, some of it quoted above, in Meres's *Palladis Tamia* (1598).

THE BEST APPROACH

Hippocrates' first apothegm states, "Art is long, but life is short." Even Solomon complained of too many books. One must be, certainly in our time, very selective. Shakespeare's ipsissima verba (his very words) should of course be studied, and some of them memorized. Then, if one has time, the golden insights of criticism from the eighteenth century to the present should be perused. (The problem is to find them all in one book!) And the vast repetitiousness, the jejune stating of the obvious, and the rampant subjectivity of much Shakespearean criticism should be shunned.

Then, if time serves, the primary sources of Shakespeare's era should be studied because the plays were not impervious to colorings imparted by the historical matrix. Finally, if the exigencies of life permit, biographers of Shakespeare who distinguish between fact and guesswork, such as Marchette Chute (Shakespeare of London), should be consulted. The happiest situation, pointed to by Jesus in Milton's *Paradise Regained*, is to bring judgment informed by knowledge to whatever one reads.

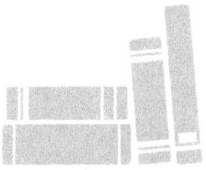

INTRODUCTION TO THE TEMPEST

GENERAL

The Tempest, although it is one of Shakespeare's shortest and most compressed plays, is perhaps the most difficult of all to analyze and interpret. The play defies analysis, and as it is endlessly suggestive, it has given rise to more than its share of odd interpretations. Often it has been seen as a religious or historical allegory, sometimes upon the flimsiest of evidence. It is equally as often identified with Shakespeare's own life and especially with his farewell to his art and to the English stage. The survey of critical opinion concerning this play that is provided in the present work will point out some of the more extreme interpretations; the student is advised to weigh these carefully before he accepts any of them.

Before we begin the scene - by - scene study of *The Tempest*, it is in order, then, at least to point out some aspects that are particularly interesting or puzzling in the reading and interpretation of this play.

THE UNITIES

Structurally, the most important thing about *The Tempest* is that for once Shakespeare adhered rigidly to the three unities of classical drama, which had been described by Aristotle, his followers, and especially by Horace, the Roman satirist and literary theorist.

The three unities were those of time, place, and action. In most of his plays Shakespeare was lax in observing the unities, and therefore it has sometimes been thought that in *The Tempest* he observed them in order to show his friend and critic, Ben Jonson, that he was capable of doing so if he wished.

The unity of time was a concept that specified that in a play all of the action should be confined as closely as possible within the course of a single day. Extreme purists even insisted that the playwright should follow reality even more precisely and have his play last exactly as long as the action on the stage, with no time lapses at all. It would seem that *The Tempest* covers no more than four hours, because there does not appear to be the interval of a single night. Note also throughout the play that Shakespeare makes constant references to the passage of time in such a way that he makes the time element conspicuous.

The unity of place is easily perceived. Everything takes place on a supposedly deserted island, except the storm in Act I, Scene 1; but then this storm takes place so close to the island that it really qualifies under the concept of the unity of place. And this unity is exceptionally well observed in the play. Finally we come to the unity of action. This means that no irrelevancies should be permitted in the course of the play and consequently all subplots and digressions should be avoided. Shakespeare has something of a subplot in the persons of Stephano, Trinculo, and possibly Caliban, but at the same time these are all tied together by the plot against the master of the enchanted island, Prospero.

The original purpose of the three unities, which Aristotle and his followers at first simply described and did not absolutely prescribe as necessary, may well have been an increase in artistic verisimilitude - or the quality in virtue of which a work of art convinces us, at least temporarily, that it represents true reality. Since *The Tempest*, among all of Shakespeare's plays, is the most fantastic and improbable on the surface, employing as it does many elements of magic and the supernatural, the observance of the unities here helps the audience to suspend its disbelief in the marvels that the play presents, as though they were everyday occurrences.

THE MASQUE ELEMENT IN THE TEMPEST

There is a well - known element of masque in the play. This means that there is a great deal of singing, dancing, supernatural machinery, and overall a feeling of romantic unreality. But a masque (see E. Welsford, *The Court Masque*, listed in the Bibliography), also implied an anti - masque, which was usually a dance of satyrs or other clumsy and fantastic personalities. This is where Caliban comes in, because he and the other characters of the subplot of *The Tempest* represent and anti - masque approach. A banquet was also common material in a masque, and its vanishing was another piece of stagecraft for the wonder and amusement of Shakespeare's audience. Within the play *The Tempest* a wedding - masque is performed, in Act IV at the betrothal of Ferdinand and Miranda.

DATE

The Tempest is generally dated in 1611. It is known that it was performed at the English court to celebrate the marriage of the daughter of King James I (who reigned 1603-25), the Princess Elizabeth, to the County Palatine, or the Elector of the Palatine, who was a German prince of the time with headquarters in Heidelberg. The marriage is dated 14 February 1613 (new style). The play celebrates fertility, and thus it is interesting to note that while the Elector and his wife sat on their thrones for a brief period and then spent the rest of their lives in exile, they did a great deal for the royal houses of Europe, providing many inheritors of thrones and dukedoms. But the first performance of the play seems on good authority to have been at court in 1611.

SOURCES

There are a number of possible sources for the play, none of which is absolutely established. Interestingly enough, one source of the play involves the founding of America (see Section III of the Bibliography, which deals with the sources); one book, *Shakespeare and the Founders of Liberty in America* (1917), by Professor Charles Mills Gayley, especially deals with this source.

A boat carrying Sir George Somers, Admiral Sir Christopher Newport, who was one of the first founders of Virginia, and Sir Thomas Gates, the new Governor of the Virginia colony, was lost en route from Plymouth to Jamestown. It was cast away on the Bermudas (the "still - vexed Bermoothes" of *The Tempest*) on July 28, 1609. The shipwrecked men built a new, smaller boat and sailed to Virginia. Subsequently the adventure was reported back in England, leading to the publication of Silvester Jourdan's account of the wreck called *A Discovery of the Barmudas*, otherwise called the *Isle of Divels* (1610). There is also another account, by William Strachey, dated July 15, 1610 though apparently not published until 1625; it is very possible that Shakespeare saw the latter account in manuscript form.

Silvester Jourdan was actually a member of the crew of the Virginia - bound ship, called The Sea Adventure. It is thought, further, that the character Caliban comes from the essay of Michael de Montaigne called Of the Cannibales; this possibility is discussed later. Hakluyt's *Voyages and Principal Navigations* is also a possible source, as is a play known as *The Fair Sidea* (Die Schone Sidea), written by the German playwright Jacob Ayrer sometime before 1605. But none of these may be called the major source of *The Tempest*.

ALLEGORY AND THEME IN THE TEMPEST

The outstanding and quite useful studies which deal with the basic meaning of the play are those by Theodore Spencer and E. M. W. Tillyard; these are referred to in the Bibliography. This is not to say that none of the other books and articles cast any light on the play, for some are very useful.

It has been suggested that one of the major **themes** of *The Tempest* is the growth of the human spirit, and this interpretation seems to carry an element of common sense, if made in the light of what is known today about traditional Elizabethan ideas on moral philosophy and what our age calls psychology.

Shakespeare's contemporaries felt that man's soul had, briefly, three faculties or parts: sensible, rational, and intellectual. These ideas are traceable back at least to the ancient Greek philosophers, especially Plato and Aristotle, as well as to ancient religious teachings within the Judaeo - Christian tradition.

Note the order of the three parts of the soul. It may be suggested that Caliban, Stephano, and Trinculo, represent the lowest, or sensible level of the soul (sensible - pertaining to sense - experience, lacking much intellect). The various courtiers, along with Ferdinand and Miranda, may possibly be equated with the higher, or rational faculty. Finally Prospero, with his principal servant, Ariel, may be equated with pure intellect, or that highest quality of the soul that is found in man at his best, and in the higher reaches of existence: in the angels, for example.

If the above interpretation is accepted, we would have an allegorical play showing the defeat and subduing of the two lower powers of the soul by the all - powerful one of intellect. However, Shakespeare does not carry this out completely. There are other, similar analyses of the meaning of *The Tempest*, and it is probable that in the light of what relatively recent scholarship has discovered about the way the Elizabethans and their immediate successors looked at man's nature, this kind of interpretation is probably the correct one. Of course, it must be kept in mind that Shakespeare was also writing simply to entertain, on various levels of sophistication; as is usual in his plays, there is something in *The Tempest* for almost every possible audience.

Much of the interpretation of *The Tempest* centers about the character of Prospero, and that of his two strange servants Ariel and Caliban. Prospero is so much the director of all characters and all events on the enchanted island that he is continuously before the audience - or his presence does not vanish, for he affects everything and everybody in the action of the play. (A detailed discussion of what Prospero's character may mean is provided in the Character Analyses section below.)

With these preliminary considerations about *The Tempest*, we are ready to turn to the detailed summary of the play, with the accompanying commentary.

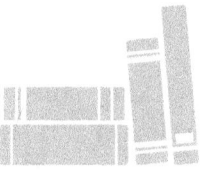

THE TEMPEST

TEXTUAL ANALYSIS

ACT I

ACT I: SCENE 1

The play opens in the midst of a violent storm at sea, with thunder and lightning. In the midst of the storm there is a ship, furiously driven by the wind and rain, and the entire first scene takes place on the deck of this ship, which is in danger of sinking at any moment.

The Master of the ship calls his Boatswain, who as the subordinate officer in charge of the sails and rigging, is directly responsible for immediate action, to make every effort to save the ship. The fury of the storm is such that it might drive the ship onto a shore where it could be wrecked; therefore, the Boatswain calls upon the sailors of the crew to "fall to't yarely," that is to say: work as hard as you can to take in the sails. It should be remembered that this storm, which we learn later in the play is supernatural in origin, has come up very suddenly, and the sailors have not been prepared for it.

As the sailors do all they can to take in the sails and make the ship secure against the storm, Alonso, King of Naples, appears on deck with his son, Ferdinand, who is heir to the throne of Naples; they are accompanied by Antonio, Duke of Milan; Sebastian, the brother of Alonso; and Gonzalo, an honest adviser and councilor to Alonso.

Alonso advises the Boatswain to "Play the men." The word "play" here has been interpreted as "ply," which would mean that Alonso is ordering the Boatswain to make the men work; it is implied that Alonso and the other passengers are not prepared to trust the skill of the officers and sailors of the ship.

Comment

With the very first lines of the play, two pairs of opposites are suggested which will be very important for the meaning as it is developed later. These are:

1. Tempest, or Storm - as opposed to Calm.

2. The Power Of A King - as opposed to Other Kinds Of Natural Or Supernatural Power.

The first pair is easy to understand, as it is represented on the stage physically. The second arises from the fact that Alonso, the King, attempts to give orders which he has no business giving. He is a King, yes, but on board a ship he is just a passenger and he must of necessity entrust his life to those whose business it is to sail the ship.

The furious activity of the crew in attempting to save the ship and the lives of all within it, at first does not impress Alonso and his friends. The Boatswain only wishes that they would get out of the way and go back to their cabins. "You mar our labors," he tells them. The Boatswain adds, speaking to Gonzalo: "What cares these roarers for the name of King?" that is, the winds and waves of the storm will certainly not listen to the King if he should tell them to be quiet, and therefore the King and his party should go below and leave the sailors to do their proper work of fighting the storm. The conversation with the Boatswain makes this clear.

Comment

The Boatswain tells the King and his companions that if they have "authority" over the winds and waves, then he, too, will obey them. Otherwise, while the King may be King on land, the order of nature on board the ship tends to make everyone equal in fighting for his life, and power to command can go only to those who have the proper skill. This point is important, and we will encounter it all through *The Tempest*, for much of the play is about power: its use and abuse.

There is some ill feeling between the sailors of the crew and their passengers; thus, as the Boatswain shouts his orders and tells the King and his party to get out of the way, Antonio says to the Boatswain: "We are less afraid to be drowned than thou art." But Antonio does not trust the crew's skill, and shows it. On the other hand, Gonzalo seems to accept whatever happens philosophically; he is even mildly humorous in his reference to the Boatswain as having a complexion "of perfect gallows." That is, Gonzalo says at several points that it is obvious to him that the Boatswain looks like a man fated to die by hanging. Since the Boatswain will be hanged upon a gallows on dry land, he cannot die by drowning. In the circumstances, this is Gonzalo's idea of a joke.

Suddenly the sailors come in wet, shouting that all is lost and that the only thing anyone can do now is to pray. Antonio is angry; he believes that the crew has not done enough. "We are merely (that is, simply) cheated of our lives by drunkards," which means that Antonio believes that the crew has been drunk and not capable of doing its best. As Scene 1 ends, the sailors are shouting that the ship is about to split apart and sink. Gonzalo has the last word when he says: "The wills above be done! But I would fain die a dry death." "The wills above" refers to the will of God or of the divine powers who, in the terms of the play, watch over and are responsible for man's destiny. But at the same time, Gonzalo can wish that things might be different on board this ship which is evidently sinking.

Comment

The idea that what happens to man is in some way supervised or controlled by a higher power, is raised at the end of Scene 1 by Gonzalo, who in many ways is a spokesman as far as the basic meaning of the play is concerned. At the same time, Gonzalo implies, man has both a will of his own and the power and duty to act to help himself. This idea is also developed in later scenes of the play.

SUMMARY

> By this short scene of only sixty - three lines, Shakespeare has brilliantly brought the reader or viewer of the play into the midst of the action, and has raised suspense to a high pitch as we wonder what will happen to those on the ship. At the same time, various pairs of opposing ideas or concepts have been introduced - important for the meaning of the play. To review these:

1. Tempest, or Storm as opposed to Calm.

2. The Power Of A King as opposed to other kinds of Natural Or Supernatural Power.

3. Fate as opposed to Man's Freedom To Act In Order To Save His Life.

4. Man (or the Human) as opposed to Nature (or The Elements or that which is Non - Human)

5. These opposites are only hinted at in the initial scene. But there is one final idea even more shadowy than these: that is, the Tempest itself is more than merely a physical storm at sea. In some way, it comes to reflect a certain disarrangement and disorder in the human spirit; therefore, there is a fifth pair of opposites which we can find in Scene 1:

6. Order as opposed to Disorder.

The order is in man himself, in the assembly of men into a state governed by a King or ruler, and in Nature. These are the three important aspects of Shakespeare's universe as described in this play; the important point to remember is that as *The Tempest* opens, all three are in a state of disorder.

ACT 1: SCENE 2

The second Scene, which composes the rest of Act 1, is very long; it takes place entirely in Prospero's cell, or small room and library where he practices his magic arts, on the enchanted island where most of the action of the play is set. The scene opens with an explanation of the origins of the storm. Miranda, daughter of Prospero, establishes her merciful character at the beginning as she asks her father, the creator of the tempest, to make the ship and all its people safe. She too is afraid all on the ship will be drowned. For Miranda has seen the ship, and as "O, I have suffered/ With those that I saw suffer . . ." she wishes those on the ship to be shown mercy.

Prospero reassures his daughter. Those on the ship will not be harmed; nobody on the ship will suffer "so much perdition as an hair," that is, will not lose even a single hair from his head, so careful is Prospero of their safety as he works his magic on them.

Prospero then explains to Miranda who she is, and who he is. It becomes obvious that until this day she has not known their origins or how they had got to the enchanted island. He removes his magic garment, apparently a costume that Prospero wears when he is practicing his magic. Reassuring Miranda: "Wipe thou thine eyes; have comfort" he explains the mystery of their origin.

The explanation proceeds by question and answer, in such a way that the audience, as well as Miranda, becomes aware of the history of both Prospero and herself. They are also told of the history of Antonio, as well as that of Alonso, both of whom we saw on the ship.

Antonio is Prospero's brother, having taken the position of Duke of Milan away from Prospero, and having exiled both Prospero and Miranda to the island. Miranda makes it clear that in the past she has often wondered who she was and where she and her father had come from, but until this day her father had always put her off with excuses. Now Prospero will tell her.

He explains that twelve years previous to this day - the day of the tempest, that is - Prospero was the Duke of Milan and held the position now occupied by his brother Antonio. He recalls the days "in the dark backward and abysm of time" when Miranda, as she vaguely remembers, had many servants and attendants, as did he. Miranda would have been so young that she wouldn't remember much of what had happened. Prospero reassures her that he is in fact her father, and that he had been exiled to this lonely place with his daughter, by the treachery of Antonio.

Prospero recalls that among all the "signories" (the states of Northern Italy), the Duke of Milan, himself, had been the greatest and most powerful. But because he studied the liberal arts and became a master of many arts and sciences, he thereby took less and less interest in the governing of his Dukedom. He gradually turned over more and more of his power to his brother, Antonio. One day Antonio, this "false uncle" of Miranda, having secretly removed many of the men whom Prospero had appointed to positions of power in the government, took over the government himself in all but name. He acted as ruler while Prospero still had the title of Duke.

Antonio's ambition grew; "he needs will be/ Absolute Milan," that is, he wanted to be the Duke. This meant that he began to plan a way to get rid of his brother. (A King or Duke is sometimes called by the place which he rules, thus, Antonio is sometimes referred to simply as "Milan" rather than as "Duke of Milan.") The exercise of power, then, gradually corrupts Antonio, as his ambition is not satisfied; he wants to have all of his brother's power.

For Prospero, as he himself says, his library "was dukedom large enough." He withdraws from the world of action and of the governing of men, into the world of ideas. His brother comes to despise Prospero's abilities as a ruler, and makes an arrangement with Alonso, the King of Naples, "so dry was he for sway" (meaning: How thirsty Antonio was for power), whereby Antonio, in return for help in taking over the Dukedom of Milan, will pay homage to the King of Naples and acknowledge his power.

Miranda, in asking her father whether Antonio could really be his brother since he has done such a terrible thing, implies that any brother capable of acting in such an unnatural way is no real brother. Here we see the idea of nature as opposed to the unnatural, which is developed further in the play.

One night, after the agreement between Antonio and Naples has been concluded, Antonio opens the gates of Milan to an invading army. Antonio, the King of Naples, and their soldiers dared not harm Prospero and Miranda, because the people of Milan all loved Prospero:

. . . they durst not So dear the love my people bore me; nor set A mark so bloody on the business . . .

Instead, they put the father and daughter to sea, in "a rotten carcass of a butt." (The "butt" is apparently a small boat, without masts or sails, in such poor repair that it is leaking.) Antonio assumes that his brother will never be seen alive again. But Gonzalo, the noble courtier and adviser to Duke Prospero, had saved their lives by placing both food and water, as well as clothing, books, and other necessaries, on the fragile boat in which Prospero and Miranda were set adrift by their enemies. At this point, Prospero breaks off the story he is telling to Miranda. By his magic art, he puts Miranda to sleep, and then summons his attendant Spirit, Ariel.

Comment

Act I, Scene 1, lines 1-187. *The Tempest*, with a total of 2064 lines, is Shakespeare's second shortest play; only *The Comedy of Errors*, with 1777 lines, is shorter; this may be contrasted with *Hamlet* (3931 lines), and *Richard III* (3619 lines). With this compression, the play must succeed in catching the audience right from the start. In this regard, the first scenes of *The Tempest* are outstandingly successful as drama.

The first part of Act I, scene 2, continues the **exposition** of the play begun in scene 1. The **exposition** is really an explanation of what has occurred before the beginning of the action of the play: its main purposes are to inform and to catch the audience's interest. If the **exposition** is successful, the audience or the reader of the play is carried so quickly into the action that he does not even realize that he is being let in on the story.

But telling the reader or audience what has happened in the past and is happening in the present is poor drama, and is not nearly as good a technique as showing or implying through action what has happened. Shakespeare is, of course, a great master of dramatic **exposition**. In *The Tempest*, as in *Hamlet*, he surpasses himself.

It is necessary for Shakespeare, in *The Tempest*, not only to tell us the story of Alonso, Sebastian, Antonio, the shipwreck, Prospero, Miranda, Ariel, and Caliban, but he must also in the first scenes of the play lead us to accept for the moment the illusion of enchantment and fantasy and magic in which the play is set. Therefore, he begins with a real event, such as his contemporaries would recognize: a shipwreck. From this, he leads us to the cell, the small room on the island where Prospero has his books and from which he controls the destinies of all the other characters in the play. Prospero's power is a fantasy, not a "real" situation or quality, but the point is that the difference between the "real" and the fantastic is so gradually shaded in that we are not aware of this difference. Therefore, Shakespeare, in this scene, leads us to believe in the existence of the island on which Prospero exercises his magic, and this is of great importance to the effect of the play.

Having made the above observations about the transition, in this scene, from reality to fantasy, we now proceed to meet the character of Ariel, who is pure fantasy.

Ariel appears at line 189, returning to his master, Prospero, in the latter's cell. This is also part of the **exposition**, and in this part of scene 2, we learn through Ariel's report to his master that he, Ariel, under the orders of Prospero, has caused the tempest. Further, it is made clear that while Prospero and Ariel deliberately frightened the sailors into believing that the ship was sinking, yet none of them was harmed. Ariel, as a spirit, had leaped on to the ship and had "flamed amazement"; he had turned himself into flames, making eerie noises, and frightened the sailors so that some of them, believing that "all the devils are here," fell, or jumped overboard. One of the first to leave the ship was the King's son, Ferdinand.

We learn further that all of the men are safe: "Not a hair perished." Indeed, not even their clothing is wet. The ship itself has by magic power been safely docked in a sort of cove or harbor, with most of the crew "charmed . . . under hatches stowed." The rest of the fleet, believing the King's ship lost, has gone sadly home toward Naples.

The first mention of the "still vexed Bermoothes" is made at this point (line 229). We shall return to this later, but it is thought that *The Tempest* was partly inspired by the account of a voyage to Bermuda. "Still vexed" means "ever vexed, or troubled," "still" being an Elizabethan meaning for "always" or "ever." But whatever places are referred to in the play, one must remember that the actual place and its geography are not important. Shakespeare sets the action in an enchanted island, where the normal laws of Nature do not operate or, at any rate, seem to be modified by the enchantments and the magic arts of Prospero and those Spirits who assist him.

We realize, as Ariel makes his report to his master, that the time is "at least two glasses," that is, about two o'clock in the afternoon. Prospero, upon learning the time, says to Ariel that between the present and the time when his, Prospero's, work ends, he must have finished what it is his intention to finish. As Prospero says (lines 240-241)

The Time 'twixt six and now Must by us both be spent most preciously.

Comment

Act I, scene 2, lines 189-241. The action of the play begins at the time of the afternoon when an Elizabethan play would actually begin to be performed, say at London's Globe Theatre, and it will last until six, or the late afternoon, for Prospero's plan is that his work will be concluded by six.

The Tempest is unique in this matter of the time - sequence, as in many other respects among Shakespeare's thirty - seven plays. It is the only play that observes the "unity of time." The tempest arises on the ship at two o'clock in the afternoon; by six o'clock everything is over. As you study other plays of

Shakespeare, in none of them will you see this feature. *Hamlet* implies the elapsing of a number of months from beginning to end of the action; *The Winter's Tale*, some seventeen years.

Just as *The Tempest* is one of the most fantastic and unbelievable of Shakespeare's plays, so Shakespeare, by his use of the most "realistic" time - scheme possible, helps us to suspend our disbelief in the strange nature of the events we are witnessing on the stage. In the course of the dialogue between Prospero and Ariel, we will learn other strange facts about this curious servant of Prospero.

At line 242 and following, the dialogue informs us that Ariel desires freedom from Prospero. Ariel is a servant of Prospero and is bound to serve him for a definite number of years. Prospero, Ariel reminds him, has promised to give Ariel his freedom early, if the present work they are doing is successful:

Thou did promise To bate me a full year.

Ariel means by this that Prospero had promised to abate, or shorten, the term of his service by a year. Prospero reminds his servant that he, Prospero, had rescued Ariel from the enchantments of "the foul witch Sycorax." This reminder, and the retelling by Prospero of the story of Sycorax and her son, Caliban, is part of the **exposition** of the play. In speaking of the torment from which Prospero had rescued Ariel, he gives us much information that we must have if we are to understand the relationships among Prospero, Ariel, and Caliban. We also learn about Sycorax, who does not appear in the play. More important, we are given certain expectations as to what kind of a being Caliban is; he does not appear on the stage until he has been described and introduced by Prospero and Ariel as they discuss him.

Caliban's shape is not exactly human. Shakespeare leaves a good deal to our imagination, but apparently Caliban appears in part like a human being, in part like a fish, in part like a tortoise. Caliban is treated not as a valued servant by Prospero, but as a slave; this is contrast with Prospero's way of dealing with Ariel. Caliban is necessary in Prospero's service, but he is still a slave, "whom stripes may move, not kindness." That is to say, he can be made obedient only by the threat of stripes inflicted by a whip.

Prospero threatens Caliban with various punishments if he does not obey. At the same time, we learn much about Caliban's nature: he is resentful, and he believes that Prospero has taken away his rights:

The island's mine by Sycorax my mother, Which thou tak'st from me. (lines 331-332)

Here Prospero loses his patience with Caliban, pointing out to him that he had treated Caliban well until he, Caliban, betrayed this kindness by attempting to attack Miranda, an attack that Prospero had prevented. Prospero had taught Caliban language and useful arts:

I endowed thy purposes With words that made them known. (lines 356-357)

But Caliban does not appreciate this, and still struggles against his master.

Comment

Here, in the relationship among Prospero, Ariel, and Caliban is raised one of the key issues of *The Tempest*, as far as understanding the play is concerned. Each of the three characters is either less or more than a literal human being; they all have special qualities and powers that we accept as part of the machinery of the play. But what do these three characters, so closely related in action, mean? We will ask this question a number of times, in different contexts, in considering *The Tempest*. Most people viewing the play in the theatre or reading it have concluded that they must have a meaning beyond the merely literal, and beyond the fact that all of them, especially Ariel and Caliban, are good entertainers.

Ariel gives us, as we are introduced to him in his scene and all through the play, an impression of lightness and lack of physical substance. He has many unusual qualities, which he uses in the service of his master, Prospero. The interchange between Prospero and Ariel, beginning at line 240 of this scene, is part of the **exposition** of Ariel's character. We learn that Ariel wishes his freedom; in this he is similar to Caliban, although in other respects he is quite different.

One of the abilities of Ariel, which we accept by this time, even though it is objectively fantastic, is his ability to travel anywhere almost instantaneously. Prospero makes this clear when he reproaches Ariel for his complaints:

Dost thou forget From what a torment I did free thee? (lines 250-251)

Ariel answers, rhetorically, "no," whereupon Prospero continues to punish his servant verbally:

Thou dost; and think'st it much to tread the ooze Of the salt deep, To run upon the sharp wind of the North, To do me business in the veins o'th' earth When it is baked with frost. (lines 253-257)

The purpose of this interchange is twofold: first, it provides additional **exposition** for the drama, so that we will know what the action has been prior to the actual chronological beginning of *The Tempest* with the shipwreck, and second, it builds up the character of Ariel so that we suspend our disbelief in such a fantastic creature.

It is best not to be too literal in one's analysis of Ariel. In the speech of Prospero quoted just above, we find that Ariel has the ability of traveling within three of the four "elements" or fundamental substances that Shakespeare and his Elizabethan contemporaries believed to constitute the material universe: Earth, Water, Air, and Fire. Ariel can move in the "salt deep"; he runs upon the "sharp wind of the North"; he serves Prospero "in the veins o'the'earth." The elements referred to are obviously Water, Air, and Earth. As to Fire, Ariel changed himself into ire to terrify the sailors in scene 1, and as we shall see, that is the element which is most akin to Ariel's own nature.

In contrast to Ariel, Caliban is a creature of the earth, earthy. Remember that Prospero specifically addresses Caliban as "Slave! Caliban! Thou earth thou!" (Act I, scene 2, lines 313-314). As one reads the entire second scene of Act I, the contrasting natures of Ariel and Caliban become more and more apparent. But both natures - and this is most important - need in some way to be guided, restrained, led or managed by Prospero. The threats that Prospero uses against Ariel are of a less menacing or physical nature than those he uses against Caliban, but in dealing with both of his servants the point is that Prospero must use threats. Prospero is, however, a kindly man, a beneficent authority - figure, and we are somehow not fully convinced that he would really put into action the threats he utters against Ariel and even Caliban.

Prospero once again reminds Ariel of "the damned witch Sycorax" from whom he, Prospero, had rescued Ariel - from her spell, that is, that caused Ariel to be confined in a pine tree. The reference to "Argier" (Algiers), from which Sycorax had been banished for her witchcraft, is one more geographical reference that shows the fantastic nature of the enchanted island. Algiers and Bermuda are not exactly close geographically, and yet the island where *The Tempest* is set seems to be in proximity to both - which is one more sign that you are not to take the geography in it seriously.

Having recalled Ariel to his duty - not that Ariel seriously contemplated defying his master - Prospero goes to Caliban, while Ariel departs in the shape of a water nymph. The entire dialogue between Prospero and Caliban, lines 321-376, is interesting in a number of ways. First, it establishes further the character of Prospero, and tends to confirm our view of him as one who is the master of everything and everyone on the enchanted island. Second, it gives something of Caliban's history and establishes his character so that we can see why Prospero treats him as he does. Caliban is at once a rather humorous creature, of indefinite shape, and a creature who has elements of pathos as well as comedy. He reproaches Prospero for having stolen his land: "This island's mine by Sycorax my mother. . . ." (line 331). The Elizabethan age was, of course, an age of discovery and exploration. English mariners such as Drake, Hawkins, Frobisher, had contributed their share to the explorations, and it was natural that reports of strange and wonderful lands and people, both real and exaggerated, should find their way back to England in Shakespeare's time. Caliban in part comes from these reports of exploration, and we shall discuss this aspect of his portrayal in additional comments on this scene.

Prospero reproaches Caliban for having attempted to "violate the honor of my child," that is, Caliban had attempted to attack Miranda. Prospero, of course, having total power on the Island, could foil this attempt. He says that Caliban was ungrateful because he had been taught language by Prospero, and had repaid evil for good. Caliban replies that the island was his by right of inheritance, and that Prospero had simply taken it from him by superior force and cunning. But Caliban recognizes, as we learn at the end of the dialogue between Prospero and his slave, that he has no choice but to obey - for he says of Prospero:

His art is of such pow'r It would control my dam's god, Setebos, And make a vassal of him. (lines 373-375)

The god, Setebos, does not appear in the play, but the name and quality of this being have some importance as showing how Caliban is initially ruled by the darkest superstition. Part of the action of *The Tempest* involves the education of Caliban as well as of most of the other characters. But Caliban, as a semi - human serio - comic character, has farthest to go in the matter of education.

Comment

Students may be interested in reading Robert Browning's poem "Caliban Upon Setebos." Of course, the great 19th Century English poet's dramatic monologue was written much later than *The Tempest*, but the student may find the interpretation of Caliban's character in this poem to be useful in the reading of the play.

The scene changes to another part of the Island to reveal the shipwrecked son of the King of Naples; he has just come ashore from the wreck, and believes his father to be drowned. Suddenly hearing the strange and fantastic music, including the famous song "Full fathom five thy father lies..." Ferdinand is led by Ariel to a point where Prospero and Miranda meet him. Ferdinand realizes that he is in the midst of enchantment:

This is no mortal business, nor no sound That the earth owes. (lines 407-408)

Ferdinand is the first man, other than her father, whom Miranda has ever seen. She believes him to be a god or a spirit, but Prospero reassures her that he is a man, who has human senses and qualities. But Miranda artlessly gives her heart to Ferdinand almost from the moment she sees him. This is exactly what Prospero intends:

It goes on, I see, As my soul prompts it. (lines 419-420)

This statement by Prospero, spoken as an aside, is the first hint we have that everything that is to take place on the enchanted island, beginning with the meeting between Ferdinand and Miranda which Prospero intends shall end in their marriage, is at the will of Prospero, who is in perfect control of everything, and everybody: human, supernatural, and elemental, on the Island.

If Prospero intends Ferdinand to be his daughter's husband, one may reasonably observe that he does not show this in his initial treatment of Ferdinand. What is Prospero's motivation for his rough treatment of the young man who has already declared his wish to make Miranda the Queen of Naples?

Remember that Miranda herself is ignorant of men and of the world. She cannot, in order to be properly valued by her future husband, appear to be too easy a conquest. Ferdinand must win her, and Prospero intends that he do so by passing a kind of test. Therefore, he accuses Ferdinand of coming to the Island to spy, and in addition, of being an usurper:

Thou dost here usurp The name thou ow'st ["ow'st" means "ownest"] not, and has put thyself Upon this island as a spy, to win it From me, the lord on't. (lines 453-456)

Technically, Prospero would seem to be making up a story to test Ferdinand. But in a deeper level Prospero's charge contains an element of truth. Ferdinand is an usurper. He is the son of a man who had assisted in the usurpation of Prospero himself. And usurpation - the act of taking away the power of a lawful King or Prince - was considered not only a grave crime, amounting to treason, by the Elizabethans; it was also considered by many to be a religious offense, amounting to impiety or blasphemy. The whole question of the powers and duties of a King or Prince is examined in this play, and we shall have more to say about it hereafter. For the moment it should simply be pointed out, so that as you read the play you will pay particular attention to the speeches on government and Kingship, or the art of ruling well.

Ferdinand emphatically denies Prospero's charge that he is on the Island as a spy: "No, as I am a man!" (line 456). Here, in this short phrase, another opposition or contrast is set up by implication: man's nature and attributes. To put it another way, one of the pairs of contrasting values or qualities that the play stresses may be illustrated as

Man against The Non - human The Inanimate The Beast The Less - than - human The Supernatural

All of the qualities or kinds of beings opposite to man have slightly differing values. But it should be clear that when Ferdinand calls himself a Man he is assigning to the word values that are not all readily apparent. A Man - a true one - cannot be a spy or a traitor.

Theodore Spencer, *Shakespeare and the Nature of Man*, 2nd ed. (New York: MacMillan, 1958), is highly recommended as supplementary reading for *The Tempest*.

Miranda tries to plead for Ferdinand:

There's nothing ill can dwell in such a temple. If the ill spirit have so fair a house, Good things will strive to dwell with't. (lines 457-459)

But Prospero pretends to be hard and sternly resists his daughter's pleas. He proposes to manacle Ferdinand and to make him do hard labor like a common convict. When Miranda continues to intercede for Ferdinand, Prospero rebukes her:

What, I say My foot my tutor? (lines 468-469)

That is, Miranda, his daughter, is subordinate to Prospero in all things; he is her head and can tell her what to do, by the laws of relationship between parents and children. A relationship in which Miranda could prevail over her father and tell him what to do would not be natural, or according to what Shakespeare and his contemporaries would have called the Law of Nature. Prospero prevents Ferdinand from resisting by placing a "charm" on him, which prevents him from moving at all, so that he stands in a frozen position. He says that Ferdinand is so possessed with guilt, that is, a guilty conscience for being a "spy" and "traitor," that he does not dare to strike with his sword. Prospero further says to Miranda that she has been deceived by Ferdinand's appearance only because she has never seen other men; that Ferdinand is inferior to most:

To th'most of men this is a Caliban, And they to him are angels. (lines 480-481)

Ferdinand has no choice but to give in and do what Prospero commands; he says in a brief soliloquy that he would sooner be imprisoned so long as he can see Miranda once a day than be free anywhere else in the world. To this, Prospero comments as an "aside" that "It works" (line 494). This means that the spell that Prospero has used - or rather, the "charm," is working - and also, the growing affection between Ferdinand and Miranda, which Prospero hopes will culminate in their marriage, is working as he wishes.

Ariel has been standing by, carrying out Prospero's commands, for he, Prospero, seems to work by the agency of his various servants, rather than directly. Prospero praises him and reminds him that if he does good work he shall be free. As the long scene ends, Miranda speaks to Ferdinand, excusing her father's apparent rudeness and lack of hospitality to a shipwrecked guest. Prospero orders Ferdinand to follow along, to the place where Prospero will put him to work, and once again, as the scene ends, cautions Miranda not to speak in behalf of Ferdinand.

Comment

Several problems are raised about Prospero's character in the latter part of Act I, scene 2. First, he is, or seems to be; open to criticism for his actions in treating Ariel, Caliban, and Ferdinand rather harshly. In the case of Ferdinand, he makes a charge that Prospero knows to be false. He accuses Ferdinand of being a spy on the Island, as well as a traitor. Yet it is obvious that he plans that Ferdinand shall marry his daughter, Miranda - and he certainly would not want his daughter to marry a spy and traitor. If we grant this, Prospero then seems to "bear false witness against his neighbor." How can this be justified, especially since Prospero is supposed to be a wise, just, and benevolent ruler of everything on the enchanted island?

The answer lies in the action of *The Tempest*, which we may term "education" and "initiation" of all of the other characters besides Prospero. From Caliban to Alonso to Miranda - all seem to develop and to learn more about the nature of ultimate reality during the course of the brief action. All become educated in a higher sense. Prospero alone is unchanging, since he is already perfected at the beginning of the play. He has become master of himself, and can thus rule the others.

SUMMARY

In conclusion, we find the following important functions of Act I, scene 2, within the dramatic and intellectual structure of *The Tempest*:

1. The scene forms the major part of the **exposition** of the play.

2. It introduces us to Ariel, Caliban, and their master, Prospero, and establishes the complex relationship among these characters.

3. It is a transition scene between the matter - of - fact circumstances of "real life," as represented by the

shipwreck in Act I, scene 1, and the world of fantasy and symbolism represented by Prospero's cell and by the enchanted island. Therefore, it leads us to suspend our disbelief and to accept the fantastic world in which the action of the play occurs.

4. The plan of Prospero, involving the marriage of his daughter to the young Prince of Naples, Ferdinand, is revealed. We learn something further about the wisdom of Prospero when he determines to subject Ferdinand to a test to see if he is worthy to marry Miranda. At the same time, it is made quite clear that Prospero is in control of everything and even foresees what will happen.

5. The concept of education - the education of all of the characters in the play other than Prospero himself - is developed. All must learn about their natures and what is required of them - even Caliban learns.

6. Finally, the question of what constitutes a Man is first raised, in Ferdinand's reply to Prospero's charge that he is a traitor. Thus, whatever else the play is "about"; whatever may be said to be its **theme**, it is a play that in some way examines and analyzes the nature of man at the deepest level of analysis. It is this depth of analysis that has made *The Tempest* endlessly fascinating.

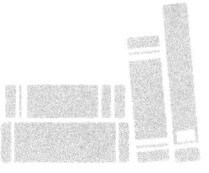

THE TEMPEST

TEXTUAL ANALYSIS

ACT II

ACT II: SCENE 1

The word - play at the beginning of this scene is interesting as a help to define further the various characters who are introduced here. Gonzalo, the old courtier, at the beginning of the scene counsels his king, Alonso, to be thankful for the escape of himself and his party from the shipwreck. This advice is in keeping with the cheerful and straightforward outlook manifested by Gonzalo in the brief first scene of Act I where he combines philosophical - religious acceptance of what cannot be changed, with a good practical streak of self - help: that the passengers and crew of the apparently sinking ship can and should do all in their power to save themselves and the ship.

Every day sees newly - ruined merchants and newly - widowed sailor's wives as a result of the sea's wrath, says Gonzalo to his master. Therefore, Alonso should be thankful for his preservation, for few in millions Can speak like us. Then wisely, good sir, weigh, Our sorrow with our comfort. (lines 7-9)

It is rare good fortune that any of the ship's passengers is still alive. But Alonso will not be comforted, because he believes his son, Ferdinand, to have been drowned. In the case of Alonso, the King of Naples, this is more than simply a personal grief, because what he manifests is deep grief for the loss of his heir, who was to inherit the throne of Naples from him. Gonzalo, whose function it is to serve and counsel his master, advises moderation, as well as submission to that which cannot be changed.

Sebastian and Antonio, on the other hand, establish themselves in a few words as rather sarcastic and cynical individuals who mock Gonzalo rather cruelly, although the old man is defenseless against their taunts and largely ignores them. The two are intent on baiting Gonzalo, but they seem to be striking beyond him at the King himself in the world - play at the beginning of Act II. Sebastian is, of course, the brother of Alonso and may be presumed to have a right to speak more familiarly to the King than anyone else could. Antonio is the brother of Prospero, the deposed Duke of Milan. At the beginning of the play, of course, Antonio is acting as the Duke of Milan, having usurped his brother's place as was recounted in the speech of Prospero to Miranda. Antonio has no idea that his brother is still alive, and indeed is the supreme ruler over the enchanted island upon which Antonio has been cast.

There is a certain balance or similarity between the situation of Sebastian and that of Antonio - with the difference that while Antonio is the present Duke of Milan (having usurped his brother), Sebastian is simply a nobleman, the brother of Alonso. But it becomes clear that what Sebastian wishes to do is to usurp the position of his brother - to depose and probably kill Alonso just as Antonio had usurped Prospero's place and had cast him adrift with Miranda.

The intentions of Sebastian and Antonio, then, are identical. The speeches that subtly attack Alonso depend on word - play: for example, in line 18 Sebastian and Gonzalo make a play on the different words "dollar" and "dolour," or sadness. It seems cruel of Sebastian to make fun of Gonzalo's comforting speech, spoken to the King with perfectly good intention. Sebastian mocks the old man, picturing him as a sort of cheap entertainer who ought to be thrown a dollar's worth of coins for his meager efforts. Alonso keeps asking the old courtier to be silent, for his grief over the supposed death of Ferdinand is too great to be borne.

Of Gonzalo, Sebastian and Antonio say:

Antonio: He misses not much. Sebastian: No; he doth but mistake the truth totally. (lines 56-57)

This is because Gonzalo has been praising the island on which they have landed; he praises it as the means of their rescue and salvation:

The air breathes upon us here most sweetly. (line 45)

So Adrian says.

Adrian is a neutral, and is thus the subject of attack by the cynical Sebastian and Antonio. The place is not good enough for them, they imply sneeringly, and this is their general attitude toward their surroundings. Therefore they think Gonzalo an old fool, and Adrian as well, judging from the cutting remarks they make.

In a deeper sense, Gonzalo is right. "He misses not much." He is in harmony with the spirit of the enchanted island, which is a healing and educative spirit or temper, as we shall see further. Another thing that the "old fool," Gonzalo, picks up more quickly than anyone else is the fact that though all the men have been in a shipwreck, their garments are ". . . rather new - dyed than stained with salt water." (lines 62-63) Gonzalo, in short, is the first to perceive that the Island is a strange and enchanted place. His reaction is characteristic: he seems to accept his new circumstances cheerfully, just as he did on board the apparently sinking ship in the first scene of *The Tempest*.

The subject of the marriage of Alonso's daughter, Claribel, to the King of Tunis, is mentioned by Gonzalo. You will recall that the ship bearing the King of Naples home from the wedding of his daughter had been the one, out of a fleet, wrecked when the tempest sprang up suddenly. Therefore, it seems a bit rash for Gonzalo to refer to the marriage, for it simply reminds Alonso of his loss - both of his daughter, by marriage, and of his son, by drowning -

Would I had never Married my daughter there! For, coming thence, My son is lost. . . . (lines 104-106)

Francisco, the other "neutral" character of the King's party, along with Adrian, reassures the King, in astonishingly vigorous poetic lines, that Ferdinand may still be alive, for he, Francisco, had seen Ferdinand strongly swimming toward the store.

To Francisco's optimism about the fate of his son and heir, Alonso simply replies: "No, no, he's gone." (line 119) Alonso is a man bowed down by grief, and there is just a hint in this scene - confirmed later - that he is also troubled by secret guilt. In some way, he may regard Ferdinand's supposed drowning as a just punishment inflicted because of his, Alonso's, offense in assisting Antonio to usurp Prospero's rightful place as Duke of Milan. This is one of the reasons why Alonso seems prepared to believe the worst, and to assume that the waves have taken his son and heir.

Comment

Act II, scene 1, thus far helps establish the characters of the King of Naples and various members of his party:

1. Gonzalo appears optimistic, rather childlike and garrulous, but never offensive. He also proves himself to be quicker - witted and more observant than the others when he perceives that although all of the people in his group have been in a violent storm and shipwreck, none shows any physical evidence of this. Incidentally, the matter of the dry clothes is one more indication that the action of *The Tempest* is to be thought of on a deeper level than merely the physical.

2. The King of Naples, Alonso, is lost in his own grief over his son's supposed death. There is a suggestion, in line with the motif of guilt and punishment in *The Tempest*, that the King regards the death of Ferdinand as a judgment imposed on him for his complicity in the usurpation of Prospero.

3. Even this early in Act II, serious questions are raised about the qualities of character of Antonio and Sebastian.

The whole question of usurpation: the deposing of a lawful sovereign, whether by violence or by intrigue, was a burning one for Shakespeare's age. Some political theorists and religious writers went so far as to say that a King or Prince must never be deposed. A corollary of this proposition was that a wicked, unjust tyrant should be borne by his people uncomplainingly because in all probability he was the "Scourge of God"; in other words, a punishment sent by God for the sins of a nation or people.

The Tempest is in part about the characteristics of the just ruler, as represented in the play by Prospero; it is also about the wise and just counselor, represented by Gonzalo. Finally, the play concerns the relationship between the ruler and those whom he rules, as illustrated in Prospero's relationship toward all of the others on the island, especially to Ariel and Caliban, and also as illustrated in Alonso's relationship to his subordinates, including the two potential murderers and traitors - Antonio and Sebastian.

Prospero and Alonso, therefore, are contrasted in the play in terms of their adequacy as rulers according to the notions held by Shakespeare's age. Alonso is tainted by having connived at usurpation, with Antonio. To the Elizabethan audience it would therefore come as no surprise to see Alonso's own life placed in danger - to see here a potential tragedy of usurpation and regicide (the murder of a King). Just as Alonso was guilty himself of complicity in such a crime, so Alonso himself may become a victim of it. This same **theme**: that once a lawful King is supplanted, there seems to be no end to the troubles of a country, is manifested also in Shakespeare's history plays, especially the so - called "major tetralogy" (the series of four great history plays including *Richard II, Henry IV* Parts I and II, and *Henry V*). King Henry IV, having supplanted and later killed the weak and erratic King Richard II, feels the guilt of his deed, and he is never fully cleared of this guilt.

Remember that during all of Queen Elizabeth I's long reign (1558-1603) there were plots against her throne, motivated by national and religious differences, for it was argued by some that as a daughter of Henry VIII by Anne Boleyn, Elizabeth had no lawful right to the throne and could justly be deposed, by force if necessary. Others saw this doctrine of the possible lawfulness of usurpation as dangerous in the extreme, perhaps leading to a civil war or a foreign invasion. We do not know Shakespeare's exact views on the subject, but as illustrated in many of the tragedies and history plays, Shakespeare's orientation seems to have been that to usurp a ruler is always fraught with danger, and that once a ruler has been deposed, no man can predict or control the outcome in the state. And this is one of the ideas examined and illustrated seriously in *The Tempest*, which is one of the factors leading to the play's usual description as one of Shakespeare's most philosophical dramas. It is, to sum up, in part a drama of political philosophy: a study of the use and abuse of power among men.

Prospero alone, on the enchanted island, has no superior exercising power over him, and needs none.

SUMMARY

Act II, Scene 1 (continued)

Sebastian, Alonso's brother, reproaches Alonso, stating that he is sure Ferdinand has drowned, because of the King's stubbornness in marrying his daughter to an African, "Where she at least is banished from your eye..." (line 121). Sebastian actually seems quite bitter towards his brother, as he rubs in the supposed loss of the heir, Ferdinand. As we shall see, Sebastian is not even sincere in this.

Gonzalo in the latter part of Scene 1 tries to be a peacemaker, to heal the grief caused by the missing Ferdinand, and in this he acts as a healer; this explains his description as a surgeon.

Beginning with line 138, we have Gonzalo's famous "ideal commonwealth" speech, in which the old courtier explains what he would do if he had "plantation" of the island - that is, if he could govern it without reference to other powers.

Comment

There is insufficient dramatic motivation for Gonzalo's speech here, that is, the speech concerning the ideal way of governing the island does not arise naturally out of the dramatic situation, except possibly from Gonzalo's wish to keep talking so that the King will forget his own grief. Gonzalo says that if he were setting up a little colony or state on the island he would abolish all contractual relationships or relationships governed by law - in fact, he would abolish all laws, all forced labor, all trade, and would go back to a sort of primitive state of nature.

The state of nature, with no compulsion or law, would "insure" that the characters of all of the island's inhabitants would be pure and upright instinctively. Man would not be corrupted by trade, and indeed would do no work. There would be no crime, Gonzalo continues, on the island; this is an utterance loaded with ironic meaning, because the audience will shortly become aware, after Gonzalo's speech, that Sebastian and Antonio are bent on the worst forms of crime: not only murder, but treason and regicide, which were crimes worse than simple murder in the eyes of most of Shakespeare's contemporaries. For regicide and treason are crimes committed not against an individual so much as against the entire people of a nation. Therefore, the state of innocence, which may admittedly be very impractical, spoken about by Gonzalo in his speech, is still in the higher sense more "practical" than the destructive plotting engaged in by Sebastian and Antonio.

Summary (Cont'd)

At the conclusion of the ideal commonwealth speech, Sebastian and Antonio, with their bitter tongues, shout "Long Live Gonzalo!" Alonso, too, asks his servant to keep quiet because the King would be alone with his grief. Gonzalo gently reproaches Sebastian and Antonio in line 176: "You would lift the moon out of her sphere. . . ." meaning that their boastful statements and their criticism of the King as well as of Gonzalo quite exceed their talents. On a deeper level of analysis, this is exactly what Sebastian and Antonio plan to do: to upset the ordinary course of nature, as symbolized by the regular cyclical movements of the moon, by committing treason and, in the case of Sebastian, fratricide (the murder of a brother).

Comment

It is well established that Gonzalo's ideal commonwealth speech, on the surface so poorly motivated dramatically, is taken at least in part from the essay, *Of the Cannibals*, by Michael de Montaigne. Montaigne (1533-1592) of course wrote widely on many practical as well as speculative subjects. The essay referred to, written originally in French, was translated by John Florio into English in 1603, so Shakespeare could have read it prior to the composition of *The Tempest*. Further, there is a copy in the British Museum of Florio's translation of the essay

Of the Cannibals, which is thought perhaps to contain a genuine signature of Shakespeare, one of the few in existence. But the signature's authenticity is not proved; if it is authentic, of course it would establish that Shakespeare had used the essay in *The Tempest*.

The tradition of an "ideal" state or commonwealth extends far back in the history of political theory, at least as far back as Plato's *The Republic*. But the enchanted island is not a Utopia or ideal commonwealth. Shakespeare implies, in this play and in others, that man is not capable of attaining directly the state of perfection in which he would exist in an ideal commonwealth. Man must first be purified by trials and perhaps temptations, and he must above all come to know himself. This Prospero achieves. Unlike Shakespeare's great tragic heroes, however, Prospero attains self - knowledge before there has been a tragic action. The situation all through *The Tempest* is potentially tragic, especially in view of the plot of Antonio, almost worthy of an Iago. But it is only potential tragedy, for Prospero keeps control of all events.

On the surface, then, Gonzalo's famous speech seems to be irrelevant, and the King quite right in telling him to be silent, for he, Gonzalo, "dost talk nothing to me," says Alonso. But on a deeper level of interpretation, the speech of Gonzalo does have meaning in terms of the play, as it relates to the problems of the governing of men, which the play raises.

The enchanted island is a place, indeterminate in space and time, which brings each being on it by the end of the play to see into himself, and to see what he is - to learn. Only Prospero has attained the stage of self - knowledge by the beginning of the play. The island, then, is a crucible in which various beings are tested.

Summary (Cont'd)

Ariel enters, line 180, playing solemn music, while he is himself invisible. By means of a "spell," or more correctly, a "charm" (the difference, as we shall see, is that a charm is the means appropriate to the kind of White Magic used by Prospero and his agents, in contrast to the spells used in Black Magic by such beings as Syrocax, mother of Caliban, who was a witch), Ariel affects all of the characters of the King's party except Alonso, Sebastian, and Antonio. Then Alonso falls asleep, leaving Sebastian and Antonio. This is not an accident, of course. It gives occasion for that which is in Sebastian and Antonio to express itself unhindered - that is, murderous intention.

Note that Antonio, Prospero's brother, the usurping Duke of Milan, is the one who takes the lead and suggests that the two should murder Alonso. Antonio, who speaks rather convincingly to his more hesitant companion, offers reasons why they should murder the King: Ferdinand, the heir, is drowned; Claribel, the King's daughter, is in Tunis, "ten leagues beyond man's life" (line 241); she is so far away that even a letter can hardly reach her. Therefore, it would be likely that with Alonso out of the way Sebastian would succeed to the throne.

Sebastian remembers in turn that Antonio had been successful in getting rid of his own brother, Prospero, but he is still hesitant:

But for your conscience - (line 270)

Sebastian means that Antonio would be afraid to commit the act of violence against the King because his conscience would trouble him thereafter. But Antonio claims that he is not bound by the dictates of conscience or abstract morality. The Good, for

Antonio, is to seize power by whatever means possible, because power is good in itself.

As Sebastian and Antonio talk, and as Sebastian seems to be won over to the latter's plan of killing the King, suddenly Ariel sings in Gonzalo's ear -

While you here do snoring lie, Open - eyed conspiracy His time doth take. (lines 294-5-6)

Gonzalo wakes, and immediately arouses the King, who wants to know why Sebastian and Antonio are "drawn" - that is, have their swords unsheathed. The answer is obvious to the audience, but not to the King or Gonzalo: the two conspirators have been surprised in the very attempt of taking Alonso's life. But neither has the sheer brazenness to murder the King or his party while they are awake; Sebastian and Antonio are fit only to murder by stealth or to kill sleeping men. On the practical level, as a matter of fact, they would probably not succeed were the King awake, as it would be four against two.

Antonio and Sebastian make up a convenient lie, that they had heard the roaring of bulls and lions. The King may distrust them already: who could know Sebastian better than his own brother? He turns to Gonzalo for corroboration of the story told by Antonio, and they are all put on guard. Gonzalo, too, may be a bit suspicious of the two secret conspirators. At the end of Scene 1, the party, swords drawn, sets off to explore the island and to see if Ferdinand can be found alive. Ariel, at the end of the Scene, having carried out the command of Prospero, goes back to report to his master.

Comment

The arch - villain of the play, according to the revelation of character that takes place in this scene, is Antonio. He is the opposite of Prospero, for as his brother is morally good, kindly, benevolent, and in command of himself, so Antonio is the victim of overweening ambition for power unaccompanied by moral scruples, as he himself says. It is Antonio who helps further to corrupt Sebastian, and not the other way around. In line 218, when Sebastian says: "To ebb/ hereditary sloth instructs me," he also says something about his situation. As a younger son, Sebastian had been kept from the throne by Alonso, who had the rulership by right of inheritance. There is an implication that Sebastian is weak, that he does not take affirmative action, and that he can be easily led.

SUMMARY

Act II, Scene 1, then, has the following purposes.

1. Differentiation of the characters of Alonso, Sebastian, Antonio, and Gonzalo, and their further establishment as individuals necessary for the dramatic exposition,

2. The humor provided by the comic or serio - comic repartee between Gonzalo and Sebastian and Antonio. Critics have perceived that this scene is by no means successful as comedy, if comedy it is at all. Shakespeare seems to be dealing with too serious a subject, and writing on the edge of comedy, moving into the area of the highest philosophical drama.

3. Gonzalo is established in this scene as an admirable and alert subordinate and counselor to the King, utterly loyal to him, in contrast to the potential traitors and murderers. Gonzalo is not of the same stamp of character as Polonius in *Hamlet*; he is more like the courtier who upholds his King to the death, namely Kent, in *King Lear*.

4. The plot against the life of Alonso is revealed in this scene, paralleling the plot that we will shortly see against Prospero.

ACT II: SCENE 2

The Scene begins with Caliban carrying a burden of firewood, as he has been ordered to do by his master. He curses Prospero, asking his, Caliban's, gods to inflict on Prospero various horrible diseases. He also tells of the tortures his master inflicts on him for his rebellious thoughts. Sometimes spirits appear to him in the form of apes, or snakes - both animals that Shakespeare's contemporaries regarded as peculiarly associated with magic and sorcery.

Trinculo, a jester, appears. His position at the court of Alonso, as the court jester, is to be a licensed Fool - he has affinities with the Fool in *King Lear* and similar characters in other plays of Shakespeare. But Trinculo is presented as a distinctly ordinary man, full of the ability to make petty mischief. It is significant for the meaning of the play that at first Caliban worships him as a god, first believing that he is a Spirit sent by Prospero to torment him. Trinculo humorously describes the fantastic half - human creature Caliban very vividly. This beginning of Scene 2 does possess genuine humor, in contrast to the forced human and repartee of Sebastian and Antonio in the preceding scene; the humor inheres in the incredulity with which Trinculo and then Stephano, drunk, view Caliban, and the comments they make about him. Stephano, a butler at the court of Alonso, enters unsteadily waving a bottle and singing a tune, a sea - chantey.

Comment

The Jester, or Fool, of whom there are many examples both in Shakespeare's Comedies and in his Tragedies, is a licensed entertainer at Court, permitted to say things with impunity which others might secretly think but which, if uttered openly, might lead to severe punishment. He is more a cheap trickster than a magician or a minor oracle, at least in the case of Trinculo. But a Jester is often the source of witty sayings - something for the groundlings to laugh at - and Scene 2 is such a scene. Added to the portrait of Trinculo is the fact that this is a drunk scene, and a drunk scene almost always gets a laugh, psychologically explained perhaps by the picture of man who has lost control of himself. Man, in Shakespeare's plays, in this situation sinks to a level below that which is expected of him.

The drunk scene, then, between Stephano, Trinculo, and Caliban, has a serious substratum, although it is very good and funny entertainment.

Stephano and Trinculo, with the quickness of street rogues, understand that Caliban is more terrified of them than they of him. Caliban, most usually presented on stage as dressed in a bearskin (because Trinculo describes him as a fish does not necessarily mean he looks like one; he can take a number of forms as presented in the actual theatre) pleads with the two scapegrace characters and arouses their curiosity. They quickly realize that they may be able to turn the situation to their own profit. They both show a low form of cunning in this. Neither of the men knows whom Caliban is talking about, when he refers to his torments at the hands of Prospero. Their reckless courage - especially that of Stephano - is the wine talking in part. Trinculo assumes that Caliban is a devil. Stephano (line 96) alludes to the proverb: "He who sups with the Devil must needs have a long spoon," and he says with bravado that if Caliban is a devil and not a monster he will leave Caliban. But much of the "bravery" shown by the two rogues is clearly bravado. It will not stand any testing - and Stephano and Trinculo are, in a half - serious way, being tested even as Alonso and his party are being put to a test, and even as Ferdinand is tested. This is not to say that Stephano and Trinculo are "serious" characters; they are not. They provide comic relief from the lofty and compressed action of *The Tempest*, which teases us into thought. But here they, too, are tested.

Initially the two are successful in fooling Caliban. Like Miranda, although at a much more primitive level, Caliban is an innocent: he has no experience of the "outside." Thus, in an aside to the audience, Caliban indicates that he thinks Stephano and Trinculo to be "fine" creatures indeed. He decides that he will worship them, as long as they do not turn out to be spirits sent by Prospero to torment him. The "celestial liquor" that Stephano brings is a powerful inducement also to Caliban.

Stephano tells Trinculo that he has a "whole butt" of the liquor (line 130); the butt, or cask, of wine has apparently been washed ashore after being heaved overboard by the sailors to lighten the King's ship which had been thought to be sinking at the beginning of the play. This fact is important for the future action because it is on "firewater" that Stephano, Trinculo, and

Caliban are going to obtain sufficient courage to attempt to kill Prospero and take over the island.

Caliban seeks a new master, then, and finds him in the rather unadmirable person of Stephano:

I'll fish for thee, and get thee wood enough. A plague upon the tyrant that I serve! I'll bear him no more sticks, but follow thee, Thou wondrous man! (lines 157-60)

Trinculo himself perceives that Caliban's trust is misplaced, as he observes that Caliban is a -

. . . most ridiculous monster, to make a wonder of a poor drunkard! (line 162)

Caliban, at the end of this Scene, exits with his new master, singing somewhat unsteadily of his new - found "freedom":

No more dams I'll make for fish, Nor fetch in firing At requiring, Nor scrape trenchering, nor wash dish. 'Ban, 'Ban, Ca - Caliban Has a new master. Get a new man. Freedom, high - day! high - day, freedom! freedom, high - day, freedom! (lines 175-82)

Comment

(Concluded) Act II, Scene 2

Shakespeare usually presents a serious meaning in a drunk scene, which is almost always good for comic effects as well. One remembers Cassio's famous remark, in *Othello* (Act II, scene 3, lines 290-94), made after he has lost his military position as a result of a drunken brawl:

... O God, that men should put an enemy in their mouths to steal away their brains! That we should, with joy, pleasance, revel, and applause, transform ourselves into beasts!

This is not to say that Shakespeare was writing a temperance tract or advising his audience to avoid strong drink. Stephano and Trinculo, after all, have been aboard ship; they have at least amateur standing as sailors, and sailors are not averse to liquor, supposedly. But in *The Tempest* a clear distinction is made between man's rational nature and his animal nature - as well as between the right exercise of man's rational faculties (as represented by Prospero), and the corruption or perversion of these faculties (as indicated in the plot hatched by Antonio). At a comic level, we see men (and half - men, such as Caliban, who cannot really be expected to do any better) descending to the level and status of beasts. Psychologically, the comic effect of this scene is considerable in terms of the "roaring" drunkenness of Stephano and Trinculo. But the underlying seriousness of the distinction between rational man and man as beast should not be neglected. Ariel, an invisible and disembodied spirit, seems to lead these characters further stray through his enchanting magic later in Act III, but it must be kept in mind that Stephano and Trinculo have the responsibility for their own actions. They are responsible human beings who are somehow degrading themselves.

SUMMARY

This short scene, Act II, scene 2, has the following purposes:

1. It develops the plot in which Caliban has to kill his master, Prospero. In this, it parallels exactly the plot that Antonio formulates to kill his King.

2. It deepens the character - sketch of the fantastic creature Caliban who, while he is human in some ways, has a poetic view of reality, as shown by the speeches he makes in this scene describing the enchanted island. Further, it shows Caliban's apparently legitimate struggle to escape from bondage into freedom; this is made clear in the last lines of the scene. It appears sentimental to say that Caliban symbolizes here the evils of slavery, or that Shakespeare protests against the institution of slavery, for such protest, historically, did not come until more than a century later. Actually, Shakespeare treats Caliban's claim to freedom with skepticism: Caliban simply exchanges a beneficial relationship to his true master, Prospero, for a new servitude to two foolish knaves. The point is that in this scene Caliban becomes a being whom we may take seriously for what he represents.

3. It further distinguishes between Stephano and Trinculo. Stephano is the more aggressive of the two, and bears the same relationship (as an initiator of plots or as a world - be ruler) to Trinculo that Antonio bears to Sebastian.

4. The scene points up a parallelism with the plot against Alonso's life, although the two plots are of unequal degrees of seriousness. For while the Stephano - Trinculo - Caliban plot against Prospero has many elements of comic relief in it, the same may not be said about the deadly serious plot of Antonio and Sebastian against Alonso.

5. Thus, one of the ultimate purposes of this scene is simply comic relief, to set against the plot against the King, the love - affair of Ferdinand and Miranda, and the spells and charms of Prospero and his servants - all of which are presented in more or less serious terms.

THE TEMPEST

TEXTUAL ANALYSIS

ACT III

ACT III: SCENE 1

At the conclusion of the preceding scene, Caliban has been deceived into believing that Stephano and Trinculo, the lowest and most roguish members of the ship's company cast up on the enchanted island, are as gods; he has been led astray by what might be called his lack of experience of mankind in general.

At a much more elevated level, in the present scene we see a process of education taking place, in which Miranda, who has been entirely innocent previously, now begins to learn more about the world, under the careful guidance of her father. In this, Miranda's state and Caliban's are similar: they both need at this point to learn more about the "outside world"; to recognize various types and characters of men, good and bad. The scene, then, begins with Ferdinand; we see him undergoing his test. This scene, in other words, forms a continuity with Act I, Scene 2 at the end, where we saw Prospero leading Ferdinand out to the place where he is going to force him to do physical labor.

Ferdinand's task is to pile up thousands of heavy logs, and he must do this under Prospero's "sore injunction" - if he does not complete the work as he has been told to do, he will suffer for his neglect.

Comment

The best explanation of Ferdinand's soliloquy at the beginning of Act III seems to be that he is happy in doing his hard work, even though it is base work, quite unworthy of a King's son and heir. But his thoughts are on Miranda, his beloved, whom he hopes to win as his Queen. So his labors are "refreshed" just by thinking about Miranda.

Miranda and Prospero enter; Miranda is visible to Ferdinand, while Prospero is invisible. Her language is characterized by startling figures of speech, quite in keeping with the romantic tone of the scene: thus she says that the log that Ferdinand is at the moment lifting will itself regret the effort it caused Ferdinand:

When this burns, 'Twill weep for having wearied you. (lines 18-19)

Ferdinand will not allow Miranda to help him with his task. It would dishonor him to do so, as she is the lady he serves. He is, in a sense, serving Miranda much as a knight - errant would serve his lady. A certain amount of comedy arises from the incongruity of the situation at the beginning of this scene: the high - flown, romantic language of Ferdinand, contrasted with his menial situation. But he is undergoing his test under the personal supervision of Prospero.

Prospero, unseen, contemplates the meeting of his daughter and his future son - in - law, and is very well satisfied. "Poor worm, thou art infected!" says Prospero of his daughter, but this is said in a tone of endearment. He means by this that Miranda has already fallen deeply in love with the Prince, which is exactly Prospero's intention, both from his concern for the personal happiness of his daughter and for reasons of state. A line from the charming short English opera Dido and Aeneas, composed by Henry Purcell in 1689, perfectly reveals the source of the special concern a King or Prince would have for the contracting of such a marriage alliance:

When monarchs unite, How happy their state, They triumph at once O'er their foes and their fate!

So it will be with Prospero, for he too will triumph over his foes when the marriage is contracted.

Ferdinand, in this impossible romantic transport of his, suddenly asks Miranda her name; he has been so enthralled by this beautiful creature that he does not even know what she is called. She answers even though her father had told her not to disclose who she is:

. . . Miranda. O my father, I have broke your hest to say so! (line 35-6)

The name "Miranda" means a female who is "one to be admired" (Latin). Ferdinand does, of course, "admire" her, addressing her as "admired Miranda" (line 37).

Ferdinand goes on in extravagant praise of Miranda while continuing to pile up the logs. Miranda tells him in turn (line 48) that she scarcely knows what other men and other women look like because she cannot remember her early childhood.

Ferdinand announces his "condition," or social status, to Miranda at this point, in lines closely involved with the political meaning of this scene. He is a Prince, and since he believes that his father is dead, he thinks that he may have inherited the throne of Naples, although he wishes it were not so. This shows Ferdinand's soundness as both a son and a Prince: he is not too impatient for the supreme power of the throne, and demonstrates true filial affection for his father.

By doing the menial work demanded of him, he feels that he "serves" his lady, and this excuses the kind of labor he must perform at Prospero's order:

I am in my condition A prince, Miranda - I do think a king (I would not so!) - and would no more endure This wooden slavery than to suffer The flesh-fly blow my mouth. Hear my soul speak! The very instant that I saw you did My heart fly to your service, there resides . . . (lines 61-66)

This is, then, love at first sight between two royal persons who immediately recognize in each other their true mates.

Miranda asks very directly and artlessly: "Do you love me?" Normally, this is not a question that one in Miranda's position would ask, for natural innocence is, in the usual way of the world, obscured by guile and indirection. But remember that Miranda is in a state of innocence on the enchanted island, quite removed from ordinary life, and therefore she does not have the defenses and the devious ways one might expect such a beautiful woman to have in the world, in Shakespeare's presentation of her. Her lack of guile is charming rather than forward or offensive.

Within a few lines, the couple have exchanged vows of fidelity and are really engaged. A mutual promise to marry at some time in the future is, for the Elizabethans, a valid engagement, and would have been so understood by Shakespeare's audience. Prospero is pleased to see this.

Fair encounter Of two most rare affections! Heavens rain grace On that which breeds between 'em! (lines 73-75)

Prospero's observation can be understood in at least two senses. First, he signifies that he is pleased by the engagement, about which he has not been consulted, though he later ratifies it and gives the couple a proper betrothal (at the beginning of Act IV).

Second, and more important, he sees "that which breeds between 'em" as not only affection, but ultimately progeny. And to one of royal blood this was most important. Prospero's line will inherit another throne, that of Naples, in addition to the one which is already Prospero's by right: the throne of Milan.

Miranda does not force herself on Ferdinand as his wife; her directness and lack of dissimulation are entirely natural to one who has had the isolated upbringing she has had. But her royal qualities manifest themselves, as do Ferdinand's.

Prospero cannot rejoice at the event as much as the actual participants, but the engagement represent the entire success of one portion of his master plan. He leaves, at the end of this scene, for he has much more to do before his plan can succeed entirely:

I'll to my book; For yet ere supper time must I perform Much business appertaining. (lines 95-7)

Comment

This scene is relatively straightforward; it shows the fruition of one of Prospero's plans. At the beginning, Ferdinand is shown doing heavy manual labor under threat of dire punishment if he fails. But Ferdinand's status as an accused traitor and spy very rapidly changes in this scene to that of the betrothed of Miranda and the future King of Naples, as well as the son - in - law of Prospero.

Again, Prospero's image is established as the man who is in control of everything and everybody on the Island. At hidden levels of symbolism and suggestion, it is made clear by hints in the play that nothing can go wrong with Prospero's plans; he is omniscient and omnipotent, with respect to the other beings on the Island. Yet at the same time, suspense must be maintained dramatically, and Shakespeare does this by a combination of the Sebastian - Antonio plot against the King and the Stephano - Trinculo - Caliban comic and drunken conspiracy against Prospero. Neither has the slightest chance of success. This scene of the betrothal of Ferdinand and Miranda represents a change in the action, then, as it is the resolution of the first thread of Prospero's complex plan, which involves the further "education" of everyone on the Island, including his daughter. The scene is an idyll, or romantic interlude. It suggests more than it states, and what it suggests, along with its golden romantic atmosphere created by the engagement of the lovers without any of the usual artifices and denials common to such situations, is the great power of Prospero to dispose the affairs of others to a good end.

SUMMARY

Act III, scene 1, has these purposes:

1. The transition of Ferdinand from a suspected traitor and spy undergoing punishment to the status of Miranda's betrothed husband.

2. The completion of one phase of Prospero's plan; this occurs with the engagement of his daughter, his heir (since apparently he has no son to inherit the Dukedom of Milan) to the heir of the King of Naples, which will strengthen Prospero's dynastic prospects, a very important consideration for Shakespeare's world.

3. The further characterization of the charming, innocent, and quite unaffected royal pair, Ferdinand and Miranda, who are presented as natural aristocrats. Their royal blood would manifest itself no matter how humble the surroundings, and this is demonstrated in this scene.

ACT III: SCENE 2

On another part of the island, Caliban, Stephano, and Trinculo are wildly drunk; this is a continuation of Act II, Scene 2. The reader should note how the stories of Ferdinand and Miranda, the most ideal, innocent, and attractive types of man and woman, are alternated and contrasted with the comic relief provided by the drunken Stephano and Trinculo and the wild man or man-beast, Caliban. The two humans who are descending to the level of beasts, along with Caliban, are found at the beginning of this scene drinking from Stephano's butt of wine.

Caliban has taken Stephano as his lord and master; he asks if he may lick Stephano's shoe, and asserts that he will not serve Trinculo, for "he is not valiant." Trinculo mocks Caliban as a "deboshed fish." Caliban offended, asks protection of his lord:

Lo, how he mocks me! Wilt thou let him, my lord? (line 29)

In the above line, "let" means "stop."

Trinculo - and here Shakespeare - makes a play on the meaning of "natural" in line 30. Natural means "according to nature," or, in the case of Caliban, a "natural" being without any spirit or soul - merely a part of nature. "Natural" also, as a noun, means one who is an idiot or imbecile; a fool. But Caliban turns out to be more intelligent and more "human" than either of his two companions, so in this sense he proves himself to be not a "natural." A monster is by definition unnatural, so this is a play on words - the kind of play in which Trinculo and Stephano, as well as Antonio and Sebastian, engage in. It may be significant that Prospero, the lord and master of the island, does not engage in word - play of any sort; for him, what he says is what he means, if his hearers can understand his message. For most of the other characters, words can have various serious and comic meanings which are less than straight - forward, to fit in with the character of the speaker.

Stephano drunkenly threatens Trinculo, telling him to be respectful of his betters. There is here just a suggestion that even in a "state of nature," where men exist without laws or governments, a natural authority or chain of leadership will be established; if there are even two men, one will become the master and the other the subject. This could be an implied critique of Gonzalo's ideal commonwealth speech of Act II, Scene 1.

Ariel appears at this point, maintaining invisibility by magic arts, just as Caliban says to his new master:

As I told thee before, I am subject to a tyrant, A sorcerer, that by his cunning hath cheated Me of the island. (Lines 40-42)

Ariel says to Caliban aloud: "Thou liest." Shakespeare uses this scene for comic relief, because while Ariel is invisible, his voice can be heard by the drunken pair as well as by Caliban. Stephano believes that it is Trinculo who says, "Thou liest." Accusing Trinculo of giving him the lie, he finally strikes him. Between gentlemen in Shakespeare's time, for one man directly to accuse another of calling him a liar was grounds for a duel. Here Stephano and Trinculo are presented as aping their betters, for both act as though they were kings and noblemen instead of ordinary rogues. They are examples of men acting under no restraint of lawful authority.

Ariel, then, says three times that Caliban has lied. The third time, Stephano mistakenly beats Trinculo for having said he, Stephano, has lied.

Comment

This scene, too, is very humorous as acted usually, since Stephano and Trinculo are reeling around the stage drunk. Part of the humor then arises in the perception of the two rogues pretending to be noblemen, with Stephano giving orders as though he is the feudal lord of Caliban. The serious undertones of this scene in here in the fact that it is Caliban who seems more in control of himself, more single - minded in what the three should do to wrest control from Prospero, than the two humans. Though a monster, a beast, he behaves more according to the dictates of reason than the others, and thus he becomes more of a serious character. The monster evolves in the direction of humanity, while the two men sink further toward the level of the beast.

SUMMARY

Caliban proposes to his would - be master a means whereby they can destroy Prospero and then attain the rulership of the island.

... thou mayst brain him, Having first seized his books, or with a log Batter his skull, or paunch him with a stake, Or cut his wesand [windpipe] with a knife. (lines 85-88)

The books are the key, Caliban says. Without them, "he's but a sot, as I am." This statement happens to be false, for as Prospero is presented, his power seems to have its origin in his own character, of which the books, the magical charms, the troop of Spirits who serve him, are merely an external symbolic manifestation.

Caliban then tells his new "master" about Miranda, and Stephano decides that he will make her his queen and together they will rule the island. He vows to kill Prospero and to take Miranda by force, as well as to make Trinculo and Caliban "viceroys" on the island. Finally, he apologizes for beating Trinculo.

Suspense thus is built up to a higher pitch as this plot against Prospero's life is further advanced. Ariel, who has been listening in, still invisible, says that he will inform his master.

Actually, it bears repeating that even though Ariel goes through the motions of keeping his master informed, we somehow get the idea that Prospero already knows everything - that he does not even need Ariel's assistance, although he makes Ariel think that he does need him. He is educating Ariel, too, in service, as he is educating in different ways everyone else on the island.

Ariel, rather weirdly, re - enters playing a tune on a tabor and pipe, or small drum and fife. Stephano and Trinculo, even through the fog of liquor, are terrified at the supernaturally - caused music, because they can see nobody playing. Even here, there is a distinction between Stephano and Trinculo, for Stephano defies the unseen powers:

If thou beest a man, show thyself in thy likeness. If thou beest a devil, tak't as thou list. (lines 124-5) Caliban begins to test his new master when he asks him, Art thou afeard?

Stephano replies that he is not afraid; this bravado is in contrast to the reaction of Trinculo, which is to pray for deliverance while he seems to be utterly terrified.

Another of the many speeches of almost supernaturally beautiful poetry occurs in the latter part of this scene. As in the case of the other such speeches - e.g. Prospero's magnificent speech, "Our revels now are ended . . ." (Act IV, scene 1) - the great description of the enchanted island by

> Caliban is insufficiently motivated dramatically. It simply seems to spill over from the situation, as Shakespeare effortlessly creates these lines from an excess of power and creativity:
>
> Be not afeard. The isle is full of noises, Sounds and sweet airs that give delight and hurt not. Sometimes a thousand twangling instruments Will hum about mine ears; and sometimes voices That, if I then had waked after long sleep, Will make me sleep again; and then, in dreaming, The clouds methought would open and show riches Ready to drop upon me, that, when I waked, I cried to dream again. (lines 132-139)
>
> These lines characterize Caliban as a natural apprehender of beauty, despite his misshapen form. In fact, he speaks some of the most beautiful poetry in the play.

Comment

The above speech illustrates the sound - **imagery**, or appeal to senses other than the visual, found in *The Tempest*. Professor Caroline Spurgeon, in a pioneering study of Shakespeare's **imagery**, pointed out that in *The Tempest* "It is the sense of sound which is thus emphasized, for the play itself is an absolute symphony of sound, and it is through sound that its contrasts and movement are expressed, from the clashing discords of the opening to the serene harmony of the close." (Caroline F. E. Spurgeon, *Shakespeare's Imagery and What It Tells Us*. (Beacon Press Paperback, Boston, 1958), p. 300. This study, of great use in considering Shakespeare's plays, was published in 1935.) This point may properly belong in the critical commentary on the play provided in the present study, but it is most important here. This speech is one of the outstanding examples of the auditory **imagery** in the play, and is rather incongruously set in a scene that really exists to provide comic relief. Yet the words and images spoken by Caliban are almost magical in their evocative power. Further, the musical and sound **imagery** points out once again the suggestion of one of the major tensions or oppositions in the play, the oppositions that may be diagramed as:

Order versus Disorder Harmony versus Disharmony

But we will deal with **theme** or tension in greater detail elsewhere, in the general criticism of the play.

Caliban keeps urging that Prospero must be destroyed; he is still desperate to escape the domination, or what he considers to be the domination, of his old master. As the scene ends, Stephano, Trinculo, and Caliban move off stage, to the music Ariel plays to lure them along.

SUMMARY

The purposes of Act III, scene 2, are:

1. Comic relief.

2. The continued building up suspense, especially as regards the plot against the life of Prospero.

3. The further establishment of the interesting and not altogether unattractive character of Caliban, as he transfers his allegiance from Prospero to Stephano, temporarily, as it turns out.

ACT III: SCENE 3

As Stephano, Trinculo, and Caliban go crashing off through the woods, we find the party of the King wandering about on another part of the island. We know that this party too - certainly Sebastian and Antonio - represents the deterioration of man rather than his perfection. They plot murder and treason against their King, just as Caliban and his cohorts plot against Prospero.

Gonzalo and Alonso are, in the beginning of Scene 3, tired and disheartened. Alonso's spirit is dull, for the King is now certain that his son is drowned. Antonio, again, viciously whispers in Sebastian's ear to the effect that "he's so out of hope" that it makes Antonio glad; a most unnatural statement:

I am right glad that he's so out of hope. (line 11)

Antonio means by this that since the King is so beaten down by sorrow for his lost son, he will be even easier to kill. But while this makes even clearer the picture of Antonio as the instigator of the plot, and a most cold - blooded villain, it still shows that neither Antonio nor Sebastian possesses the ruthlessness necessary to confront the King while he is awake in order to kill him. If either of them did have such courage, *The Tempest* would then have been a tragedy, not a tragi - comedy or dramatic romance. Sebastian and Antonio agree to effect their treacherous plot that same night. Suddenly, as they have concluded their agreement once again, there is strange music. Prospero appears. As it would be staged in the theatre, he stands on an upper stage, invisible to the members of the King's party. He directs various strange shapes, who bring in a banquet and dance about it, inviting the famished King and his companions to eat.

Comment

The feast, with the dance, is entertainment - another interlude in the midst of the serious business as the plot moves toward its **climax**. In terms of the allegorical dimensions of the play, it further shows Prospero's power. Magicians were noted for conjuring up illusory banquets like this, but there is a deeper allegory perceptible here: a temptation scene, or a banquet with overtones of religious sacrament and religious ritual. Sebastian and his companions are unfit to partake of the banquet, for they are, as Ariel is to say in his long speech as he appears to them, "three men of sin."

Various fabulous monsters are mentioned by the members of the King's party as they contemplate the banquet with the eyes of hunger. The fabulous creature known as the unicorn, which has only one horn; the phoenix, which regenerates itself periodically on its own funeral pyre, and which was the subject of much mythological interpretation in the middle ages and in Shakespeare's own age - these are talked of. The King and his companions are amazed; they realize what Gonzalo, the supposedly obtuse old courtier, has long since known: that a supernatural agency is at work on the island. Gonzalo stands his ground, which is another piece of evidence that we should accept him as a kindly and entirely wise old man rather than a garrulous fool. He points out that the harpies and strange shapes have very gentle manners as they go about setting the banque:

For certes these are people of the island, Who, though they are of monstrous shape, yet, note, Their manners are more gentle - kind than of Our human generation you shall find Many - nay almost any. (lines 30-34)

Prospero comments on this, from his perch of invisibility:

Honest lord, Thou hast said well; for some of you there present Are worse than devils. (lines 35-37)

He refers, of course, to those who had had a part in deposing him from his dukedom, as well as to the plotters who seek the life of the King. After further talk about the wonders of the little - known paths of the world, the party determines to taste the banquet. Alonso himself realizes that this may be a trap and that the banquet may be poisoned, but he is indifferent, "since I feel/ The best is past" (lines 50-51). By this he means that he has little wish to live, so great is his sense of loss respecting his son.

As the party is in the very act of beginning the banquet, Ariel appears dressed like a harpy (a mythical creature possessing the face and body of a woman and the wings and claws of a bird), accompanied by thunder and lightning. Clapping his wings upon the table, he makes the banquet vanish with a "quaint device," or a trick of the stage.

Comment

There is probably an element here of temptation, with some religious overtones involving sin or guilt and the punishment thereof. This is pointed up by Ariel's long speech, one of the more famous passages in the play, whose meaning has been much debated. The speech of Ariel is really an accusation, a bill of particulars, a kind of grand jury indictment of the "three men of sin." Note that the entire speech is directed only at the three: Alonso, Antonio, and Sebastian:

You are three men of sin, whom destiny - That hath to instrument this lower world And what is in't - the never - surfeited sea Hath caus'd to belch up you; and on this island, Where man doth not inhabit, you 'mongst men Being most unfit to live . . . (lines 53-58)

This implies that the members of the party are outcasts from humanity, having forfeited their status as human beings by some terrible crime that places them outside Nature, so that even the "never - surfeited sea" rejects them. Destiny has "to instrument" this lower world - this means simply that the impersonal force or power of Destiny has the earth as its instrument.

It is thus implied in this speech that there is both a lower or actual material world and a higher or ideal world; this is basically a Platonic notion that would have been quite familiar to Shakespeare and his contemporaries. By plotting murder, usurpation, and fratricide, as well as treason, the members of the King's party have conformed not to the ideal but rather to the lowest and most brutal aspects of the lower world. They have incurred guilt, which must undergo purgation and purification. Thus Alonso, Sebastian, and Antonio are also being tested and tried, even as was Ferdinand, though in the latter case his testing was briefer and less harsh.

Both Alonso and Sebastian draw their swords at this point. Ariel mocks them for doing so:

You fools! I and my fellows Are ministers of Fate. . . . (lines 60-61)

They have no material substance. How, then, can Ariel and his agents be hurt by the swords? Ariel casts here, by Prospero's power, a charm on the guilty men so that even if they could use the swords they are now unable to lift them. Ariel, at this point, recounts the specific crimes, primarily centering around the charge that the three:

From Milan did supplant good Prospero. (line 70)

Here the loss of Ferdinand is tied up with the punishment for this offense of usurpation, as it has been earlier in the play. Alonso now knows what his guilt is, though he has sensed it earlier. During the time while Ariel is speaking, the party appears paralyzed, as in a trance.

The grammatical structure of this whole speech is complicated, but essentially it means that Ariel, as one of the ministers of fate, is called upon to be an avenger of Prospero, and that the fates have pronounced on the three "lingering perdition," meaning that the characters must undergo a purgation of their guilt leading to "a clear life ensuing" - a life free of guilt. At this point we are doubly sure that the play has as one of its important **themes** that of purgation and purification from guilt.

In the final portion of Scene 3, Ariel vanishes to the accompaniment of praise for him and his performance from his hidden master, who sees all. The shapes put on a dance with comic overtones: perhaps mocking the hungry men further as they remove the table on which the feast had been set.

Now Prospero has his enemies exactly where he wants them; as he says:

My high charms work, And these, mine enemies, are all knit up In their distractions. They are now in my pow'r . . . (lines 88-90)

But it has been clear from the action of the play that Prospero has been in control of his enemies from the very beginning, when the ship was caught in the magical tempest. Prospero then leaves to visit his daughter and his prospective son-in-law.

Alonso, staring, still partly in a trance, seems to think that the thunder has spoken to him, for Prospero appears as a vision.

. . . the thunder That deep and dreadful organ pipe, pronounced The name of Prosper; it did bass my trespass. Therefore my son i'th' ooze is bedded . . . (lines 97-100)

The tie-up between Alonso's sin against Prospero and the drowning, or supposed drowning, of Ferdinand, has been made earlier in the play in Alonso's mind: he has a conscience, and knows he has done wrong and must be punished for the wrong. Alonso is recalled to his sense of guilt. He is so overcome with remorse that he no longer wishes to live; he would prefer to join Ferdinand.

Alonso is suicidal, while Sebastian and Antonio, even more deeply marked with guilt since they have just been planning a murder, are defiant. They swear to fight all the "legions of fiends," as they exit in a frenzy of fear and defiance. Gonzalo speaks the final, and most significant lines here as the scene ends:

All three of them are desperate. Their great guilt, Like poison given to work a great time after, Now gins to bite the spirits. (lines 106-108)

This is the first time that Gonzalo has even hinted at all he knows about the guilt of the three, but obviously he knows what they have done to Prospero. Remember that at the beginning of the play Prospero had mentioned that it was Gonzalo who provided the means to save his life and the life of Miranda. So it is clear that Gonzalo knows much, yet he forgives much.

Gonzalo has a parallel with the faithful and noble servant Kent, the follower who continues to safeguard and watch over King Lear even while the King banishes him in his anger. Gonzalo likewise will look after the best interests of his master, Alonso, and follows the distracted three along with Adrian and Francisco, to see that they do not harm themselves or others. With this high point of spiritual tension the scene ends.

SUMMARY

The purposes of Act III, scene 3 are:

1. To indicate guilt and the realization of guilt in the persons of Alonso, Sebastian, and Antonio.

2. Further to advance the plot against Alonso's life and the counter - plot or counter - intrigue involving Prospero's plan to punish those who had dealt with him unjustly.

3. An illustration of the power of Prospero, presented in a way that would be appealing to the total audience of Shakespeare's day - involving such things as the dances of the strange Shapes and the antics of the harpy, Ariel.

4. It presents a sort of philosophical, hierarchical, view of the universe and of nature, with its division into the ideal higher world and the more material and gross lower world.

5. The end of Act III signals the beginning of the process of repentance and purification on the part of the King and of his guilty companions. The King is a man who is at this point mortally conscience - stricken, believing that his son has died as a direct result of his own transgression.

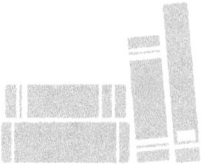

THE TEMPEST

TEXTUAL ANALYSIS

ACT IV

ACT IV: SCENE 1

At the beginning of this scene Prospero abandons the stern posture that he has taken toward Ferdinand, who has successfully undergone his period of trial and testing. His trial, incidentally, is very mild compared to those undergone by all of the other guilty characters on the Island. This points up the fact that Ferdinand has been almost entirely guiltless; he is in every way a model young man, son, and Prince, and such guilt as he may have stems from his inheritance. He is, after all, the son of a King who has participated in usurpation, and in the King's guilt Ferdinand shares by birth, but not by his own actions or inclinations. Therefore his punishment is physical only.

> . . . all thy vexations Were but my trials of thy love, and thou Hast strangely stood the test: here, afore Heaven, I ratify this my rich gift. (lines 5-8)

Ferdinand here explicitly learns from Prospero that he has been subjected to a test, and that in Prospero's view he has passed it as a King's son should. ("Strangely" had, in Elizabethan times, the meaning of "care; respectful attention.") We have seen Ferdinand resisting the imposition of the menial task at first, until he was forced to do the work by Prospero's charm, and then gladly accepting the heavy physical burdens as he convinces himself that all he does is in the service of his lady, which is in keeping with the aristocratic code by which Shakespeare's audience would have expected a King's son to behave.

Prospero, then, ratifies the gift very formally: "a third of mine own life," which probably means that Prospero has devoted himself to Miranda's upbringing for a third of his 45 years (by the chronology of the play). Prospero does not have any children other than Miranda. (See W. A. Bacon, Notes and Queries, 9 August 1947, on this subject.)

The betrothal of Ferdinand and Miranda is made quite formally. Prospero emphasizes several times the necessity for the full religious rites and ceremonies, the "full and holy rite" (line 17). Ferdinand and Miranda are sternly enjoined not to consider themselves as having the rights of married persons until they undergo the marriage ceremony. Ferdinand swears not to anticipate the delights of his appropriate wedding - day, whereupon Prospero praises him further and then calls his chief lieutenant, Ariel, to him. Ariel is to provide an entertainment for Prospero, Ferdinand, and Miranda, and therefore Prospero orders him to go and bring the "rabble" over whom he has power. These would be inferior Spirits whom Prospero can command by virtue of his white magic.

While Ariel goes away to do Prospero's bidding, the master of the Island once again warns Ferdinand that he and his bride must preserve the strictest chastity until their marriage.

Comment

The disproportionate emphasis on virginity on the part of Prospero has struck some critics as just that: out of keeping with the forgiving and reconciliatory spirit manifested by Prospero as the play develops. However, the dwelling on the subject had in all probability both a comic and a serious purpose. Wedding - night jokes or jokes especially about the bridegroom as he approaches marriage - especially its consummation - are irrepressible, and would have appealed to Shakespeare's audience much as they would to a modern audience. This is the comic aspect of the marriage.

There is more profound level or aspect of Prospero's insistence on chastity. *The Tempest* is a drama of moral as well as political philosophy; in the sphere of Elizabethan ethics and morality, it sets up the basic opposition between man's reason and his lower passions. Much of the action of the play revolves about the idea that some of the characters cast up on the enchanted island must undergo a kind of ritual purification for past guilt that they have incurred. A state of chastity may symbolize, therefore, the state of purity that is to be attained by all of the characters. Also present here is the theological concept, ultimately based on the writings of St. Paul, that virginity is a more excellent state than matrimony. Although the latter is an "honorable estate," it must be formally entered into with prescribed rites.

Beginning with line 60, the Masque presented by Ariel for the amusement of his master is acted. Iris, or a Spirit representing her, begins the entertainment. Iris is a personification of the rainbow and, according to some classicists, a messenger of the gods. She addresses Ceres, the goddess of plenty, the protectress of agriculture and also the goddess of fertility. The poetry of the speech of Iris should not be overlooked, as it conjures up effortlessly an unimaginable picture of bounty -

Of wheat, rye, barley, vetches, oats, and pease; Thy turfy mountains, where live nibbling sheep, And flat meads thatch'd with stover, them to keep; Thy banks with pioned and twilled brims, Which spongy April at thy hest betrims, To make cold nymphs chaste crowns. . . . (lines 60-66)

At the end of this speech, Juno descends. Juno was not only queen of the gods, she was also the patroness of childbirth and the protectress, as Juno Lucina, of women about to give birth.

Ceres has been summoned "a contract of true love to celebrate." Her speech, critical of Venus and of the son of Venus, Cupid, is critical because of the theft of the daughter of Ceres, named Proserpina as a result of Cupid's machinations.

The **climax** of this scene of masque and festivity, making splendid the austere cell of Prospero, occurs as Juno and Ceres impart a marriage - blessing to Ferdinand and Miranda. Prospero explains, in answer to Ferdinand's question, that the performers are spirits -

Spirits, which by mine Art I have from their confines call'd to enact My present fancies. (lines 120-22)

Ferdinand's answer is significant:

Let me live here ever; So rare a wonder'd father and a wise Makes this place Paradise.

The Nymphs enter, and continue to celebrate the marriage festivities, accompanied by Reapers. Suddenly, Prospero remembers something: the plot of Caliban and the two drunkards against his life. He dismisses the Spirits rather abruptly, and seems distracted and "in some passion," as Ferdinand observes. In fact, his daughter says that never yet has she seen him so angry. The Spirits vanish in a "strange, hollow and confused noise." At this point Prospero begins what is certainly the most famous speech in the play, and one of the two or three best-loved pieces in all of Shakespeare's work.

Comment

The masque, as entertainment, is more elaborate and contains more thematic implications than one might suppose. At first glance, this appearance and the singing and dancing of the Spirits, traditionally dressed in rich and colorful costumes, seems just an interlude. But it harmonizes completely with the healing and regenerative aspects of the enchanted island and of its master, Prospero, who indeed promotes "Earth's increase, foison [abundance] plenty."

Prospero realizes that the plot of Caliban has reached a critical point. Actually, this is an illusory statement, for Prospero has known all along what would happen and is at no time in any danger from Caliban's plot. Even his anger at the presumption of his slave in daring to plot against him seems not quite real, and not sufficiently motivated dramatically.

Speaking of dramatic motivation, Prospero's famous speech seems hardly motivated at all; it simply proceeds out of an excess of magnificent creative power on the part of the supreme English poet, and is quite beyond praise. But the question is: what is the special magic of these noble, austere, yet golden lines:

You do look, my son, in a moved sort, As if you were dismayed. Be cheerful, sir. Our revels now are ended. These our actors, As I foretold you, were all spirits and Are melted into air, into thin air; And, like the baseless fabric of this vision, The cloud-capped towers, the gorgeous palaces, The solemn temples, the great globe itself, Yea, all which it inherit, shall dissolve, And, like this insubstantial pageant faded, Leave not a rack behind. We are such stuff As dreams are made on, and our little life Is rounded with a sleep. (lines 146-158)

What called this speech forth? On the surface, simply the disappearance at Prospero's command of the airy Spirits who have been putting on the entertainment. It asserts that life is a dream, that man himself is of little more substance than the Spirits who have so casually been called up for a few minutes of entertainment and who have so quickly vanished. Further, it has long been known that Prospero's speech owes something to a **stanza** in the *Tragedie of Darius* (1603), by William Alexander, the Earl of Stirling:

Let greatnesse of her glascie scepters vaunt; Not scepters, no, but reeds, soone bruis'd, soone broken: And let this worldlie pomp our wits inchant, All fades, and scarcelie leaves behind a token. Those golden palaces, those gorgeous halles, With fourniture superfluouslie faire: Those statelie courts, those sky-encountering walles Evanish all like vapours in the aire.

The Earl of Stirling (1567-1640) was a distinctly minor Scottish poet who wrote several Senecan tragedies. Some of his lines including the aforementioned show considerable creativity, but by no stretch of the imagination could they be considered the equal of Shakespeare's verse. As a work of supreme genius, the speech of Prospero defies rational analysis. The ideas expressed in it are commonplace Elizabethan notions: that man's material life is not quite real, and that life may be described as a dream or a moment's interlude between the realities of birth and death - "the dreamcrossed twilight between birth and dying," as S. Eliot put in it in our own century. The idea of the evanescence of earthly things is an orthodox Christian idea: that at the Last Judgment the material world itself will come to an end. No doubt sermons on this topic were most familiar to the audience that saw *The Tempest*, and yet such sermons survive, if at all, in total obscurity. But Prospero's speech has outlasted and will outlast any sermon.

Comment

The speech may also serve dramatically as an implied corrective and counterbalance to the delight in the sheer physical world, which permeates the play. Even Caliban describes the enchanted island, in its physical aspects, as a delightful place, and so describes it in glowing **imagery**, as in his speech in Act III, Scene 2: "the isle is full of noises/ Sounds and sweet airs...." And Miranda, too, seems to admire the "brave new world/ That has such people in't." But the religious temper of Shakespeare's time involved at least formal subscription to the idea that everything in the physical world is vanity and will ultimately pass away: that spiritual things alone are real and unchanging.

Therefore, Prospero's speech contributes to the balance in the play between:

1. Body and Spirit 2. The Created and The World of World. Eternal Spirit. (Subject to growth and decay.) 3. Natural Fact and Supernatural Reality

Having made these observations about Prospero's speech, we have still in no way explained the unearthly beauty of these lines.

The notion that Prospero had "almost forgotten" the plot against his life is maintained. Prospero calls Ariel to him in order to arrange to foil Caliban's plot and to punish the man - monster and his two drunken associates. As Ariel describes his actions, it seems that he has led on the plotters, who have all sunk to the level of beasts:

So I charmed their ears That calf - like they my lowing followed through . . . (lines 178-79)

The three have been led by Ariel until they have found themselves in the "filthy mantled" pool of stagnant water near Prospero's cell. At this point Prospero orders Ariel to bring various brightly - colored clothes for "stale" [a decoy] to catch the prospective thieves and murderers.

Prospero once again denounces Caliban as a "devil, a born devil," who can only be trained, or rather restrained and chastised, by hard punishment. But an interesting aspect of this scene, related to the thematic content of the play, is that Caliban's punishment, as it turns out, is astonishingly light.

Comment

Prospero reflects a quite characteristic idea of Shakespeare's age when he observes of Caliban:

> And as with age his body uglier grows, So his mind cankers. (lines 191-92)

In other words, the moral condition of the soul is reflected in one's beauty or deformity of body, and vice versa: body and soul have a close relation, and ugliness of soul is often reflected in ugliness of body. Shakespeare uses precisely this idea in the play *Richard III*, and Shakespeare's contemporary, the English poet Edmund Spenser (1552-99), expressed this thought in the famous lines from his Foure Hymnes, written before *The Tempest* (1596):

> So every spirit, as it is most pure, And hath in it the more of heavenly light, So it the fairer body doth procure To habit in, and it more fairly dight With chearefull grace and amiable sight. For of the soule the bodie forme doth take: For soule is forme, and doth the bodie make. (Spenser, *An Hymne in Honour of Beautie*) lines 127-33)

This idea is ultimately traceable back to the philosophical teachings of Plato. It would not have been necessary for Shakespeare to have encountered it specifically in the above lines, for the idea, like that of the idea of the evanescence of all earthly things, was an Elizabethan commonplace.

As the three plotters approach the cell, Prospero and Ariel remain invisible, watching them. Suddenly they see the sort of clothesline upon which Ariel has hung the glistening apparel.

Caliban, showing more wisdom than his two sodden masters, tries to get them to proceed with the plot and not to be distracted by such "trash."

Let it alone, thou fool! It is but trash. (line 223)

At this point, Caliban himself is beginning to realize that he has worshiped a fool and a dullard, for Trinculo and then Stephano are easily distracted from the plot to attempt to steal the clothing. Just as they are seizing the flimsy appearances of garments, a number of Spirits appear in the shapes of dogs and hounds, with Prospero and Ariel setting them on. Prospero orders that his "goblins" grind the joints of the plotters, and rack them with cramps and convulsions. The three run off, roaring with pain, while Prospero observes that all of his plans have come to fruition exactly on schedule. As Act IV ends Prospero, speaking to Ariel - even more so to himself - summarizes the state of the action when he says:

At this hour Lie at my mercy all mine enemies. Shortly shall all my labors end, and thou Shalt have the air at freedom. For a little, Follow, and do me service. (lines 261-65)

Comment

It is important to note the difference in quality between the punishment Prospero inflicts on the three guilty noblemen, Alonso, Sebastian, and Antonio, and that which he inflicts on the three plotters who provide the comic relief of the play, Stephano, Trinculo, and Caliban.

The torments of the three nobles are spiritual and psychological. The three "men of sin" are told their offenses by Ariel at the end of Act III, Scene 3, and all of them become distracted and desperate. Gonzalo accompanies them with Adrian, to watch over them so that in their grief and remorse they will not do violence to themselves or to others. Their crimes are great, in fact, they are among the worst of which Shakespeare's age could conceive: attempted murder, regicide, fratricide, and the usurpation of a lawful ruler, or treason. The situation is fraught with potential tragedy, and if it were not for the hand of the lord of the enchanted island, Prospero, the plots and actions of the three men would certainly result in the same catastrophic kind of tragedy that is found in *Hamlet, King Lear, Othello*, and *Macbeth*. Antonio, in fact, has been likened in his unscrupulousness, to Iago, the villain of *Othello*. He could do an immense amount of mischief, were he not restrained by the unseen and wise hand of Prospero.

Thus, the three are spiritually tormented, in part by their own guilt, in part by the charm of Prospero. The King, Alonso, suffers the heaviest punishment, because in addition to the punishments inflicted by Prospero directly, the King also believes that his son and heir has been drowned. This is the worst torment of all for him, because it means (and would have so meant to Shakespeare's audience) that the dynasty of Naples would come to an end, with no direct heir available to rule. This was, as we have seen earlier, the great fear of any Renaissance ruler: that his line would come to an end, and was much on the minds of Englishmen during the reign of Queen Elizabeth I (1558-1603) and after, when the line of succession to the English throne was by no means settled.

On the other hand, Trinculo, Stephano, and Caliban have been guilty only of a comic plot against Prospero, and of the attempted theft of a few trashy clothes, as well as of the venial offense of drunkenness. They - or at least the two humans - have reduced themselves voluntarily to the level of beasts, and are so treated by Prospero, when he sets the dogs on them, just as one might do to a bear or other vicious animal. Their punishment is physical, not mental or spiritual, and therefore is much lighter than the torment suffered by the three noblemen.

The contrasts, then between the two forms of punishment should be kept in mind, Further, the purpose of the punishment, on Prospero's part, is not only correction; it is also education. And those who benefit the most from the lessons that Prospero wishes to teach are, strangely enough, those at opposite ends of the human social chain or power structure: the King, Alonso, and the subhuman monster, Caliban. We shall see this point illustrated further in the final Act.

SUMMARY

Act IV, which is not further divided into scenes, ends on a note of triumph for Prospero, as he has punished his two sets of enemies and at the same time arranged the marriage between his daughter and the Prince of Naples, Ferdinand, thus ensuring his own line of succession in Milan.

Act IV, then, accomplishes the following:

1. It brings the trial and testing of Ferdinand to a successful conclusion, further developing his character and demonstrating that he is fit to be the son - in - law of Prospero.

2. It concludes the formal betrothal of Ferdinand and Miranda.

3. It provides the semi-comic masque entertainment of June, Ceres, and other Spirits, which is thematically linked to the play's celebration of marriage, fertility, and the continuation of the royal lines of Milan and Naples.

4. The plot of Caliban, Trinculo, and Antonio is further advanced and the two drunkards are shown up for what they are, as even Caliban realizes that they are fools and that he would do better to worship other gods.

5. The scene gives occasion for some of the loveliest and most moving lines found anywhere in Shakespeare's plays, although these lines - Prospero's famous speech to Ferdinand and Miranda - seem to spring out of nowhere, dramatically.

6. Finally, the plans of Prospero are carried toward an entirely successful conclusion.

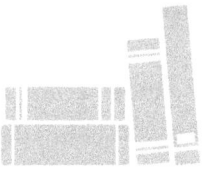

THE TEMPEST

TEXTUAL ANALYSIS

ACT V

ACT V: SCENE 1

This Act, like Act IV, is not further divided into scenes; it consists only of the relatively short Scene 1, plus the Epilogue of twenty lines of **tetrameter** verse, spoken by Prospero, which is believed by some commentators on the play to be spurious - the later addition of someone other than Shakespeare.

At the end of Act IV, Prospero had announced that all of his enemies are now completely at his mercy. However, as became clear almost at the beginning of the play, Prospero always has been in control of events on the enchanted island since the tempest began, so that nothing has changed from beginning to end of the play as far as his absolute power is concerned.

In Act V, all of the characters in the play come together in the **denouement** - the "unknotting," or events following the major **climax** of the plot of a play. In *The Tempest*, since Prospero's relative power has not changed nor has he undergone any sudden reversal of fortune, good or bad, the **denouement** of Act V is more in the nature of a final scene in which mysteries are unraveled and misunderstandings, such as the mutual belief of Alonso and Ferdinand that the other is dead, set straight.

At six o'clock - the sixth hour at which Prospero had predicted his work would end - Prospero appears in his cell dressed in his magic garments. The King and his followers are meanwhile confined in a grove near the cell; the mariners of the King's ship sleeping the sleep of enchantment, in the ship's hold. The two drunkards and Caliban are being "driven" like wild animals in the direction of Prospero's cell; and Prospero's daughter and new son - in - law, Miranda and Ferdinand, are playing at chess, oblivious to the world around them.

As Ariel describes the King, he and the two guilty lords, Antonio and Sebastian, are "distracted" and unable to move, with Gonzalo, Adrian, and Francisco watching over them. If Prospero could only see them, says his servant, his affections, or disposition toward his enemies, "would become tender." Ariel says that he would be tender toward them, were he human, which of course he is not.

Prospero's answer to the observations of Ariel is quite important for the meaning of the play, and might easily be overlooked in a quick reading:

Hast thou, which art but air, a touch, a feeling Of their afflictions, and shall not myself, One of their kind, that relish all as sharply Passion as they, be kindlier moved than thou art? Though with their high wrongs I am struck to th' quick, Yet with my nobler reason 'gainst my fury Do I take part. The rarer action is In virtue than in vengeance. They being penitent, The sole drift of my purpose doth extend Not a frown further. Go, release them, Ariel. (lines 21-30)

In other words, Prospero's enemies have repented, and therefore the Duke will not seek revenge. His reason - the faculty in man which alone he shared with the angels and with the divine principle, in the belief of most of Shakespeare's contemporaries - bids Prospero practice forgiveness rather than take the stern revenge on his enemies, which he might well take otherwise.

His enemies, then, are completely helpless in his power. But Prospero masters himself. By an effort of will, based on Prospero's long study and teaching, he resists the entirely human tendency to take revenge on one's enemies. There is an apparent change in Prospero's outlook in this speech at the beginning of Act V: he turns from revenge to forgiveness. But actually he has been bent on this course from the very beginning of the play, so the change in his attitude is only apparent. For he has foreseen what will happen from the moment he first raised the tempest, and indeed seems to have foreseen everything even before putting his plan into operation. His change of heart is as much an illusion as anything else on the enchanted island, and is employed as a dramatic device by Shakespeare to heighten suspense. The audience of *The Tempest* is left wondering, until Act V, as to the extent of the revenge Prospero will take on his enemies. After all, those enemies are formidable, especially Antonio who, as we have observed earlier, has many of the qualities of an Iago.

Comment

The ideas contained in Prospero's speech here are those of resignation, reconciliation, and Christian forgiveness of one's enemies. All were Elizabethan commonplaces, based on traditional religious teaching within what our own age might call the Judaeo - Christian ethic. The speech succeeds brilliantly not so much for the striking originality of the ideas contained in it, but rather because of the gracious and noble tone and the sheer poetic beauty of its lines.

As Ariel exits, Prospero utters the other great soliloquy of the play spoken by him - a speech almost equal in genius to the speech on the transitoriness of the "cloud - capped towers" in Act IV.

In this soliloquy, beginning as Prospero addresses

Ye elves of hills, brooks, standing lakes, and groves, And ye that on the sands with printless foot Do chase the ebbing Neptune . . . (lines 33-34)

there is at once an invocation of the magic that Prospero has lived and acted by, and an abjuration of that magic:

But this rough magic I here abjure; and when I have required Some heavenly music which even now I do To work mine end upon their senses that This airy charm is for, I'll break my staff, Bury it certain fathoms in the earth, And deeper than did ever plummet sound I'll drown my book. (lines 50-57)

Prospero ends with the requiring of "some heavenly music" that will soothe the troubled minds of Sebastian, Antonio, and the King and will awaken them free from the burden of that guilt for which they have repented.

Comment

This speech is inevitably associated by many commentators and general readers with Shakespeare's own farewell to the stage.

Shakespeare did not write another complete play after *The Tempest*; he retired voluntarily at the height of his powers, to his home in Stratford, which he had purchased after the years of fantastic creativity in London in which he had risen from the dispossessed son of a bankrupt father to an eminence as the master of his profession. In this interpretation, Prospero becomes identified with Shakespeare to such an extent that some have called this great and gravely beautiful soliloquy Shakespeare's farewell to his art; his farewell to the London stage and to the "magic" he had mastered.

At this distance, we simply cannot know whether this thought was in Shakespeare's mind or whether Prospero's speech had such an intention. Certainly the speech seems to lack dramatic motivation. The gravity of the lines, in which Prospero is saying that he will voluntarily give up his magical powers, is far in excess of what is required by the plot of the play - even as the "cloud - capped" towers speech is in excess of the requirements of the dramatic situation. About all we can say here is that it is risky to identify Prospero with Shakespeare in this speech of abjuration: there is no evidence to support such an identification, although one is tempted by the circumstances of Shakespeare's life and by the position of *The Tempest* in the Shakespeare canon to make such a comparison.

At this point in Act V, Prospero now does what his servant Ariel had earlier done in Act III: he notifies the three guilty "men of sin" of their crimes. Alonso had "cruelly used" Prospero and his daughter; Sebastian and Antonio had been "furtherers in the act" and had behaved remorselessly; and, in the case of Antonio, had acted unnaturally toward his own brother, Prospero. Both are "unnatural," because both Antonio and Sebastian would have murdered the King, a peculiarly horrible and unnatural act for Shakespeare's age.

Remarking that of course the three noblemen would not recognize him in his magical garments, Prospero calls Ariel to him once again, promising him that before long he shall have his coveted freedom, and dresses himself once again in the garments of the Duke of Milan, perhaps symbolizing his imminent return to the world and his departure from the timelessness of the enchanted island.

Comment

Here the basic Elizabethan distinction between Reason and Passion, or man's rational and his animal natures, is once again made clear. *The Tempest* is potentially a tragedy of royal usurpation and revenge: the same stuff of which *Hamlet* and *Macbeth* are made. Unbridled ambition, passion, hatred, murder, revenge, and fratricide are all present potentially in *The Tempest*. All of these negative things are dispelled and rendered harmless by the action of one man, Prospero.

Ariel's song (lines 88-94) is another of the entirely charming songs that surpass the songs of any other Shakespearean play. It is not just to say simply that they have little or no intellectual content; that is not their purpose. They are beyond the realm of the intellect.

The mariners, who have been sleeping a charmed sleep under the hatches of the King's ship, are ordered to be awakened by Ariel. Prospero presents himself to the awakening King and his company as the "wronged Duke of Milan," and embraces Alonso and Gonzalo.

Alonso, overcome, shows both disbelief at seeing Prospero and relief that Prospero is alive, for the guilt of his supposed death has weighed heavily on the King. Gonzalo, too, is overcome:

Whether this be Or not be, I'll not swear. (lines 123-24)

Prospero turns to Antonio and Sebastian and tells them that were he so minded he could denounce the two conspirators to their King and "justify" them as traitors - that is, prove that they had intended to murder Alonso. But as treason would be punished by immediate execution, Prospero promises that at least for the moment he will tell no tales. "The devil speaks in him," observes Sebastian in an aside to Antonio. Prospero's answer is interesting and not without significance beyond its shortness, for he simply says: No. It is not the devil, but the principle of divinity which speaks through Prospero.

Comment

Prospero at no time operates by the agency of the devil or of infernal powers. Whereas in *Macbeth* we find a devilish magic, or black magic, sometimes called goety, at work, in *The Tempest* we find nothing employed by Prospero except white magic, or theurgy. (The best discussion of this distinction of magics is Walter Clyde Curry's book, *Shakespeare's Philosophical Patterns*, cited in the present bibliography.)

Prospero at this point peremptorily requires and demands his dukedom from his brother, "most wicked sir." It is significant that Antonio does not even answer, as he is so filled with shame and guilt. He is, after all, the deepest - dyed of the villains in

The Tempest, and we are left with some doubt concerning the completeness of Antonio's reformation.

At this point, after Prospero's stern reproach directed at his brother (and it is significant that Prospero reserves his sternest words for that man who is clearly the most wicked among the sojourners on the enchanted island), the dramatic suspense is further built up by Shakespeare to a sort of minor **climax** where Prospero "discovers" Ferdinand and Miranda playing at chess.

This is, in the eyes of the beholders, "a most high miracle." The King is moved from despair to joy as he sees his son alive. Miranda exclaims -

O, wonder! How many goodly creatures are there here! How beauteous mankind is! O brave new world That has such people in't. (lines 182-85)

To which Prospero replies simply -

'Tis new to thee. (line 186)

This has an implication that in Prospero's view his daughter will inevitably be somewhat disillusioned by the world, which is not characterized by the wise and humane control found on the enchanted island.

Gonzalo rejoices; "Was Milan thrust from Milan that his issue/ Should become kings of Naples? O, rejoice . . ." (lines 206-7). This might seem superfluous; Prospero, having demonstrated great power over Nature herself, seems a bit silly settling for a mere dukedom again. But this signifies his rejoining of human society, strengthened by his sojourn on the enchanted island and by his studies. And his descendants will be Kings, not Princes.

A cynic might observe that at the end of the play there occurs the Elizabethan equivalent of what our own age calls "upward mobility," as Prospero marries off his daughter to a King's son. But this ending would have seemed entirely fit, proper, and fortunate to Shakespeare's audience.

Comment

Shakespearean comedy and dramatic romance ends traditionally with a marriage or the prospect of marriage. The ending of *The Tempest* follows this pattern, though it may seem relatively unsatisfactory in view of the effortless power displayed by Prospero, and the grave and stately tone of the poetry as the ruler of the island gives up his power forever to return to the care of the world. But in a deeper sense the ending is a fit one, heralding the end of one cycle of existence, represented by Prospero and Alonso, and the beginning of a new one as Ferdinand and Miranda succeed to royal power.

The scene, then, at the close of the play is triumphant because of the union of Ferdinand and Miranda, and the strengthening of the royal houses of Naples and Milan.

The ship, which "but three glasses since" appeared to be splitting - that is, three hourglasses previously - is bravely rigged and ready to go to sea again. Alonso observes that what he has witnessed must be supernatural, and Prospero promises to make clear to the assembled parties the "strangeness of this business." One practical consideration here might be simply that Prospero must demonstrate his use of white magic in his proceedings, rather than of black magic.

Prospero orders Ariel to set Caliban and his companions free, and they appear in their stolen clothing. Prospero reproaches Stephano for thinking that he could become King of the island. He orders Caliban to go to his, Prospero's, cell with his accomplices, and to "trim it handsomely." Caliban says that he will be wise hereafter:

What a thrice - double ass Was I to take this drunkard for a god And worship this dull fool! (lines 295-97)

Caliban has learned, and has advanced one step towards humanity. As the short Act V ends, Prospero promises calm seas and favorable winds, so that the ship will not only reach Naples but even catch up on the rest of the fleet, which had proceeded on, believing the King's ship lost. He charges Ariel that he attend to this:

Then to the elements Be free, and fare thou well! (lines 317-318)

As the play ends, the party enters Prospero's cell, there to hear the story of his life.

SUMMARY AND CONCLUSION

Act V accomplishes the following:

1. Obviously it is intended to tie together the threads of the story, to resolve those situations that Prospero has simultaneously been organizing and controlling on the enchanted island, and to end the play in an artistically satisfying manner.

2. The play ends on a hopeful, though somewhat anticlimactic note in this scene, with the prospective union of the royal houses of Milan and Naples likely to strengthen both realms. The scene thus accomplishes the transition back to the world, with its cares, its strivings for power, and its inevitable disillusionments. Just as the first scenes of the play skillfully lead the audience to accept with a willing suspension of disbelief the conditions of the enchanted island, so the last scene dispels these illusions, further pointing up the dreamlike quality of the play.

3. The last Act assembles all of the characters on the stage, and ends with an atmosphere or tone of reconciliation, pardon for offenses, hope for the future through the younger generation, and affirmation of the essential wonder and beauty of the "brave new world."

4. The Epilogue, composed of twenty **tetrameter** lines spoken by Prospero, is generally considered to be far inferior to the rest of the play. The lines are probably spurious, written by someone other than Shakespeare. They duplicate, though at a far lower level of poetic excellence, the lines beginning with line 33 in Act V, in which Prospero renounces his magical powers.

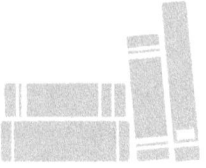

THE TEMPEST

CHARACTER ANALYSES

PROSPERO

Prospero, of course, is the play. His presence is felt continuously, even in those scenes in which he does not appear personally. He is the manipulator of the action of the play, and occupies the center of the stage very markedly, especially if one compares his position with that of the central characters of, say, most of Shakespeare's history plays. For in the latter plays, England itself becomes the hero - the English crown, in its resistance to civil war and factionalism, and therefore there is usually no one character of quite the same stature as Prospero.

In Latin, the name Prospero would mean, "I hope for." That which a member of English Renaissance society would generally have hoped for would be salvation, in the terms of Christian theology. Another meaning of his name would be "prosperity," implying that everything which he attempts will prosper. There is certainly a **connotation** of hopefulness in his name.

Prospero is purified intellect. He is a "white" magician; he practices theurgy, not goety. (Consult the chapter, "Sacerdotal

Science in Shakespeare's *The Tempest*," in Professor Walter C. Curry's book cited in the Bibliography.) By the practice of white rather than black magic we mean that Prospero's magic is always turned to good ends, and that he seeks only good. At the end of the play Prospero seems somewhat to abdicate his role as the embodiment of pure intellect, as he returns to Milan to resume his role as an active chief magistrate, or Duke.

The question then arises: is Prospero a renegade to the status he has throughout the play - the status of pure intellect? For an answer, we must turn to the concept advanced earlier in this study: that everyone on the enchanted island, including even the man - monster Caliban, learns and is educated further by the experience of the tempest and its aftermath. That the island is a place of education and learning - not necessarily formal book - learning, but rather learning to see more deeply into reality - is an axiom in the interpretation of this play. It might be better to describe the process the characters all go through as initiation, not simply education.

The point is that Prospero also learns. While he is master all through the play, he has learned well before its opening that a Prince cannot abdicate his responsibilities. It will be recalled that Prospero had lost his Dukedom in Milan in part because he neglected his everyday duties in favor of his more abstract and theoretical studies. A Prince, Duke, or King cannot abdicate his responsibilities. Prospero had been wrong when he had tried to do so, and in a way had himself been punished by exile. But during his exile he has mastered both his own nature and his surroundings, and has learned what his duty is as a ruler. He is doing only what he should when he resumes his position as the ruler of Milan. In other Shakespearean plays, any ruler who abdicates or surrenders power, such as *King Lear* or *Richard II* - especially if he surrenders power voluntarily as did Lear -

always comes to grief, and his act may lead not only to his own destruction but to the ruin of the political order of the state, as nearly happens in *King Lear*. The theory of kingship held by many Elizabethans implied that once God had appointed his viceregent in the person of a ruler, it was not for the ruler to attempt to modify God's judgments. So Prospero learns, and guided by his new and hard - won knowledge, returns to the world of Milan, where "every third thought" shall be his grave. This last probably means that he will think of eternity, of his salvation, even while fulfilling his role as Duke, for he has learned on the island that the exercise of power for its own sake is nothing.

Is Prospero a tyrant? He has been described as such by a number of critics, but in the terms of the moral philosophy embodied in *The Tempest*, he is not. He suits his attitude, his response, and even his tone of voice, to the person or being with whom he is dealing, whether it is Ferdinand, Ariel, or Caliban, or his own daughter. This is not tyranny; it is the prudence and the control of people and situations that a wise Renaissance ruler would have been expected to demonstrate, and Prospero is every inch a ruler.

Prospero may be an allegorical figure, but only to a certain extent; we can never fully delimit his allegorical meaning. He triumphs through his practice of white magic, and in effect Shakespeare shows us the triumph of good over evil; of goodness so absolute and so well - informed that it can render even the blackest plots of a villain like Antonio harmless.

Prospero embodies not only the triumph of good over evil, he also figures forth the triumph of the master of the intellect over the lower faculties of man. His long stay on the island, it should be noted, has not resulted in his becoming embittered. He has managed to achieve power over the elements themselves by the study and mastery of magic books. This seems far - fetched. If one visualizes Prospero as a great scientist or physician of today, performing wonders unimaginable in Shakespeare's times, the great powers of Prospero become less fantastic.

It may be that Shakespeare, in having Prospero admit that he is absent - minded in forgetting the plot of Caliban and his companions against his life, is emphasizing the human quality of the Duke. If he were entirely a supernatural and intellectual creature he could not forget - but the "forgetting" is, after all, a dramatic device.

As a final point about the character of Prospero, it is well to observe that Shakespeare has performed the difficult feat of making supreme goodness more interesting than supreme evil.

Prospero is entirely good: wise, just, and humane. Despite his apparent harshness toward Caliban, he really gives even the man - monster a second chance to learn, to become more human, as he allows (for nothing happens on the island but by the permission of Prospero) Caliban to see his two drunken companions for what they are during the progress of the plot against Prospero's life. And he punishes Ferdinand "austerely," but solely to test him. His goodness is manifested in many ways, yet he rarely bores whatever audience he may have, and indeed he fascinates us with his power and his magical manner of exercising it.

Although Prospero drowns his book and forswears magic at the end of the play, he has really changed little except to have become a better ruler than he was when, in "the dark backward and abysm of time" he so lost touch with his realm that he was cast away by his usurping brother. While the play really has very little spectacular action, Prospero keeps that action under effortless control throughout.

MIRANDA

Prospero's daughter, who is an entirely charming and unspoiled princess. She is artless; having no experience of the world, she does not know how to pretend or to dissemble, especially with regard to her emotions. She seems to have a minimum of contact with the supernatural forces employed by Prospero, as she evidently never sees Ariel in his own shape, whatever that is. Miranda keeps falling asleep, but there is the hint that her sleep is a charmed one, brought about by Prospero so that he can speak with his supernatural servants. Miranda, though she is his daughter, does not share his power over the elements and the supernatural.

Her artlessness in showing her love for Ferdinand is especially charming, while her name, as we have observed, means "worthy of admiration," which she certainly is by reason of her beauty, innocence, and tender consideration for Ferdinand and the other rare creatures who inhabit the brave new world she has found.

GONZALO

In some ways the most interesting of the non - supernatural characters in the play. He corresponds to the nobleman Kent in *King Lear*, in his devotion to his King, Alonso. Though an old man, he is still very alert, as witness his observation right after the shipwreck that the clothes of his companions are still dry and whole. While the other characters may occasionally bait him and think of him as a garrulous old fool, he is far from that. Even his Ideal Commonwealth speech, tangential though it may seem to the situation at hand, is intended immediately by him to cheer up his King and distract him from his grief over the supposed death of his son and heir. Gonzalo is, then, the type of the good courtier or adviser to rulers, who places his master's good above any possible personal advantage, and who even tries to protect his master from himself, as he does during the scene in which his guilt has made Alonso, the King, temporarily deranged.

ALONSO

The King of Naples, is initially a guilt - ridden man, stricken by such grief for the supposed loss of his son, Ferdinand, in the shipwreck, that he scarcely wishes to continue living. He is not presented as an especially forceful ruler, as otherwise he might contrast favorably with Prospero, which is no part of the play's intention. Prospero is the central figure, and certainly not Alonso.

Alonso had been guilty of conniving with Antonio in the usurpation of Prospero from the dukedom of Milan. This is the basic fault or offense for which he is apparently punished, or feels he is punished, by the loss of his son. But Alonso feels genuine remorse and wishes to expiate his guilt. At the end of the play he is genuinely glad to see Prospero, the man whom he had wronged, so that he can make amends. He is the most thoroughly reformed and ennobled character of all in the play. We are not sure about Antonio's reformation, but we have little doubt about Alonso's.

FERDINAND

Alonso's son and heir, the Prince of Naples, and a paragon of a young prince. He upholds an almost impossibly romantic ideal of chivalry and honor, behaving like a Prince even while, for the sake of his lady - love, Miranda, he performs the most menial of tasks. Basically a student as well as a man of action who has the martial spirit expected of a Prince, he becomes fascinated with his prospective father - in - law's magic. He is properly respectful toward Prospero as well as toward his own father, and simply by what he is inspires such confidence that we imagine the realms of Naples and Milan will fall into good hands when Ferdinand and Miranda succeed to the throne. Ferdinand is indeed gallant, and in every way will be a fit and proper husband for Miranda.

SEBASTIAN

'as seen the throne of Naples go to his elder brother, Alonso. Sebastian impresses us as rather weak and easily led; he falls under the domination of the crafty Antonio. He is potentially capable of treason, regicide and fratricide as he enters into the plot proposed by Antonio to murder the King, Alonso, in which case Sebastian would succeed to the throne. He seems more reformed at the end of the play than does Antonio.

ANTONIO

The false Duke of Milan, who had viciously usurped the place of his brother, Prospero, and had set Prospero adrift in a leaky boat with his infant daughter, hoping that they would drown. He is so "unnatural" that he would murder his own brother, without remorse, in order to gain power. He is an evil counselor, and thus is contrasted with Gonzalo, whom he mocks for an old fool. He talks the much weaker Sebastian into a plot designed to take the King's life. At the end of *The Tempest*, Antonio says nothing when Prospero requires his Dukedom back, and we are not sure how far his reformation extends. Antonio, in his unscrupulous brilliance and willingness to act decisively though in a bad cause is potentially one of Shakespeare's major villains, approaching the qualities of Shakespeare's supreme villain, Iago.

ARIEL

An incorporeal Spirit, whose true shape is never revealed but who has the ability to be everywhere and to assume various forms, such as that of a bird, a harpy, etc. He moves easily through the four elements recognized by the Elizabethans - he appears as a magic fire at the beginning of the play, in the shipwreck; he moves instantly through the air and the water; he can even move under the earth. He must be restrained continually by the sternness of Prospero, because what Ariel most seeks is freedom. He had originally been freed by Prospero from the black magical enchantment of Caliban's mother, "the foul witch Sycorax," who had imprisoned Ariel in a pine tree. Ariel is insubstantial, purely a Spirit. His origins are in Neo - Platonic teaching as well as in some aspects of traditional Christian theology and speculation concerning the various orders of supernatural beings. He is Prospero's executive arm; he manages the other Spirits employed by Prospero, and at the end is set free, to return to the elements. His is an important part in the play; more important than the parts of most of the humans in it, as a matter of fact.

CALIBAN

As Ariel is delicate and incorporeal, so Caliban is gross and close to the earth. He is a fantastic man - monster, of indeterminate shape, variously described as a moon - calf, a tortoise, and a wild man. He has brutish desires, and had sought to violate the honor of Prospero's daughter even though Prospero had at first taught him language and in other ways been his teacher. Caliban has a grievance, as he fancies that the island is actually his by right of succession and inheritance from his mother, the witch Sycorax. Yet paradoxically Caliban is a poet; his speeches describing the enchanted island are at times hauntingly beautiful. He worships a cruel god, Setebos, who might be described technically as an anthropomorphic deity (a cruel sort of god invented by men and actually reflecting some of the worst qualities of men; a god created in man's own image).

Caliban develops during the play, to the point where he recognizes the excellence of his master when he contrasts it with the sodden and foolish drunkenness of Stephano and Trinculo. He resolves to seek for grace, and to be wise hereafter; at the end of the play, he sees Stephano and Trinculo for what they are, and therefore he has learned.

Caliban's character is actually a complex blend of demonological lore of Shakespeare's time and the pure poetic imagination. He is extremely superstitious, and full of fear at what his master will do. Yet his character is by no means without appeal, and he is far from simply being an embodiment of evil. To say that Caliban is purely evil is an oversimplification.

TRINCULO

A Fool or Jester in the Court of the King of Naples, Alonso. Displays a low form of cunning, and is always ready to turn a situation to his own advantage. He is undone by his greed, when he and Stephano, roaring drunk, are led on by Ariel and the other Spirits to the point where they attempt to steal the glistening clothing from the line outside Prospero's cell. The character of Trinculo provides some comic relief within the serious action of the play, and would have been perfectly comprehensible to Shakespeare's audience, especially to the groundlings.

STEPHANO

A drunken butler, also a servant of Alonso. Stephano is more aggressive than Trinculo, and it is he whom Caliban worships until he learns better. He is distracted, as is Trinculo, from the pursuit of his plot on Prospero by the glistening clothes placed on the clothesline outside Prospero's cell; it is at this point that Caliban realizes the unworthiness of Stephano who would be so easily turned from his purpose by "trash." Stephano is not simply drunk, he is roaring drunk.

ADRIAN AND FRANCISCO

Both are noblemen who, with Gonzalo, are attendants of Alonso. They are neutral characters, hardly distinguished one from another and with very little to say. Neither is implicated in the plot against Alonso on the parts of Sebastian and Antonio. The accompany Gonzalo as he cares for the distracted King after the charm placed on him by Prospero's magic.

Iris, Ceres, And Juno are supernatural beings who appear in the masque in Act IV for the delight of Ferdinand and Miranda. They have no particular character other than the mythological, but they have more than a comic purpose, for the masque is enacted in praise of marriage and fertility, and in some way all three represent fertility - deities.

The Nymphs And Reapers are also mythologically - based beings called up by Prospero's art to join in the marriage - masque in Act IV.

The Master Of The Ship, The Boatswain, And The Sailors are seen only at the beginning and the end of the play. They are rough but entirely competent in their profession of seafaring, and are of course baffled by the magical tempest and by the enchantments that surround them. While they are all minor characters, the conversation during the tempest, when the boat is believed to be lost, is important as it sets up the problems of authority, rulership, and responsibility with which the play deals, as the King's immediate noble servants would interfere with the mariners in their struggle to save the ship.

THE TEMPEST

CRITICISM

GENERAL

It is impossible to cover even a majority of the problems raised by this endlessly suggestive play. The materials listed in the Bibliography and Guide to Further Study of the Play, while not exhaustive, will provide a good start toward a deeper understanding of the play or toward more intensive consideration of particular aspects of it.

Some earlier commentators on the play, characteristic of their centuries, were Dr. Samuel Johnson in the 18th Century and Samuel Taylor Coleridge in the nineteenth. Johnson wrote in 1765 that the "System of Enchantment" that supplied the marvelous things found in the romances of the middle ages had to be understood if one were to understand the character of Prospero as a magician. Johnson was not the first critic, nor was he the last, to see in Caliban simply "brutality of sentiment," even though Caliban's perceptions approach the highly poetic. A more cogent observation of Dr. Johnson on the play concerned the character of Gonzalo, which was that of a good man - "the only good Man that appears with the King."

Coleridge, on the other hand, avoided rationalistic analysis of the Johnsonian sort to concentrate on the "almost miraculous" qualities of the drama. He was an originator of what seems to us to be the commonplace view that the play appeals primarily to the imagination. In the 19th Century, in general the ideas were accepted that *The Tempest* was (1) an allegory and (2) Shakespeare's personal farewell to the English stage. There is evidence for both but as has been shown, neither can be fully documented. The biographical approach was intensified by Edward Dowden, who in his *William Shakespeare: His Mind and Art*, divided Shakespeare's life on the basis of his production of plays into four periods, which Dowden called:

In the Workshop In the World Out of the Depths On the Heights

Without going into the details of what seems today to be an overly romantic and undocumented explanation of Shakespeare's career, we may say that Dowden assigned *The Tempest* to the final, serene period of Shakespeare's creativity when, having emerged from the despair and darkness of his great tragic period, he was at peace with himself and with the world, and could thus produce the calm reconciliation and the forgiving spirit of *The Tempest*, and could say farewell to his art with the same nobility with which Prospero said farewell to his magic. At any rate, Dowden is thoroughly characteristic of the romantic biographical approach to the play.

THE SUPERNATURAL

One important consideration in approaching this play is the supernatural structure, with the use of magic on the part of

Prospero. It is known that belief in demons and witches was woven into Elizabethan and Jacobean society in a way very difficult for us to imagine It was not necessary for Shakespeare's audience to believe literally in magic and in the objective existence of witches and monsters, although some of the audience undoubtedly did. Indeed, several controversies raged in England over the objective truth of demonology - King James I himself was involved in one such controversy, as illustrated in his book *Demonologie* (1597), an answer to a book by Reginald Scot, *Discoverie of Witchcraft* (1584), in which Scot, actually somewhat of a rationalist, took the view that all or most alleged cases of witchcraft or of demonological phenomena were frauds. Actually, as Professor George Lyman Kittredge pointed out in his book *Witchcraft in Old and New England* (1929), "the belief in witchcraft was practically universal in the 17th Century, even among the educated."

The two plays of Shakespeare that make most use of magic and witchcraft as contributing to their very structures are *The Tempest* and *Macbeth*; in general it is white magic or theurgy that is at work is *The Tempest*, leading to a good end, while in *Macbeth* the thane of Glamis and Cawdor is entrapped, though his will always consents to the entrapment, by the arts of black magic or goety. Professor Walter Clyde Curry, whose book *Shakespeare's Philosophical Patterns* (1937) has been mentioned before, has studied both plays in this matter, and his Chapter entitled "Sacerdotal Science in Shakespeare's *The Tempest*" is extremely useful in the consideration of the play. It may be of interest that it was not until 1736 that English law was changed so that thereafter it was impossible to prosecute a person in any court in Great Britain for "Witchcraft, Sorcery, Inchantment, or Conjuration."

ALLEGORY

Allegorical interpretations of *The Tempest* are many. In general, in allegory there is a one - to - one relation or ratio between a character or event in literature and some other object or meaning; thus, as James Russell Lowell worked out the allegory of this play, Ariel was equated with fancy, Caliban with brute understanding, and Prospero with the imagination. Some allegorical interpretations seem on their face to be much too rigid; thus Colin Still parallels the action of the play allegorically with the practices of the Eleusinian mysteries and initiation rituals of the classical period, in his book cited in the Bibliography. But such an approach appears wrong - headed, for lack of real evidence.

An even more extreme criticism was that of Miss Emma Brockway Wagner, who saw *The Tempest* as an "allegory of the Christian Reformation." Each character in the play, in this view, had a part in standing for an event in the progress of Christianity throughout a total of twelve centuries, from 325 Again, there is no evidence in the play for this interpretation, and it is alluded to here simply by way of cautioning the student or reader against being carried away by the infinite suggestibility of the play.

Professor G. Wilson Knight, in *The Shakespearean Tempest* (1932) and *The Crown of Life* (1947) gave rise to some fruitful suggestions about the meaning of the play from an allegorical point of view, although at times he, too, seems to be extreme. For Knight, the play becomes a "myth of the national soul" of England, in terms of England's instincts for rulership and her political toleration, her "inventive and poetic genius," and finally her colonizing activities, which led to the upgrading and the salvation of primitive peoples. It can be seen that Knight would equate allegorically Prospero, Ariel, and Caliban respectively with these qualities. But the importance of Knight's criticism is in its suggestiveness, and his attempt to equate Prospero with an actual symbol is not as well supported as it might be by evidence.

LEVELS OF REALITY

The two relatively recent studies of Shakespeare which have been pointed out previously as being of great significance for the understanding of this play are E. M. W. Tillyard's *Shakespeare's Last Plays* (1938; reprinted 1951), and Theodore Spencer's *Shakespeare and the Nature of Man* (1942). These cannot be overlooked by any serious student of the play. Professor Tillyard develops the view that the final dramatic romances of Shakespeare, *Cymbeline, The Winter's Tale*, and especially *The Tempest*, supplement and indeed complete the pattern of tragedy found in the great Shakespearean tragedies. It is Tillyard who emphasizes the **theme** of regeneration and reconciliation in *The Tempest*, and who is more responsible than anyone else for the idea that the play starts out as potentially a tragedy, for he finds that "Antonio is ... one of Shakespeare's major villains," fully capable of causing the same kind of tragedy caused by Iago or the daughters of King Lear. Tillyard also discusses the "planes of reality" in *The Tempest*. But it is Professor Spencer who goes further in pointing up the operation in the play of three hierarchical levels of Nature: animal, human, and purely intellectual (again, levels identified respectively with various sets of characters in the play). It is he who applies the terms sensible, rational, and intellectual to the levels of being of the play, and he is convincing as he relates these levels to "the common psychological assumptions of [Shakespeare's] time."

Thus, in the approach of Professor Spencer, Caliban represents the level of mere sense, or the animal level; the plotting noblemen the level of untrustworthy reason (Antonio, after all, acts on an intellectual although certainly not on a moral level); and Prospero with his chief servant Ariel represents the level of "uncontaminated intellect." The play does not represent the final triumph of goodness, but it does show good triumphing over evil; there is an element of redemption, a re-birth or return to life after spiritual purgation, and an affirmation of life especially through the fertility - ritual elements in the drama centering about the new generation, Ferdinand and Miranda. There is also the element of illusion and reality in the play. Ariel and Prospero work up the semblance of a storm, a wreck, drowning, a banquet and a masque. But the real world obtrudes at the beginning of the play, though the audience is rapidly removed from it, and it is something to which all return at the end as Prospero embraces his duties in the world once again. The question is raised as to the metaphysical distinctions in the play between illusion and reality.

THE ABUSE OF REASON

One point that has not been made so far here is that the more villainous art dangerous plot is developed by Antonio and Sebastian, men who evidence a high order of the development of the rational faculty. Antonio is no fool; he is rather brilliant, but he adopts what Shakespeare's age would have called the Machiavellian view that the only reality is power and physical force. As long as he can get what he wants in the way of power and prestige, he will not be bothered by the stings of conscience. Sebastian is but a weaker copy of this imperfect pattern. Caliban, on the other hand, appears at the start as basically animalistic, and yet paradoxically he learns and becomes better. He is not a man, and is not expected to operate at the same high level of rationality that one would expect of a nobleman such as Antonio; therefore, he actually rises morally superior even to Antonio and Sebastian, although this may be taking too serious a view of Caliban. He is a humorous character as well as one to be taken seriously.

It is likely that some of the allegorical elements here mentioned have an objective existence in the play, although it is not primarily a religious allegory. If it were, Prospero would not return to the "real" world of men; at the same time, he shows awareness of the world of eternity especially in his speech on the illusory nature of the "cloud - capp'd towers." The play, then, if we may return to points made earlier, is centered more on man and his nature than on the supernatural; it deals with order in the life of man, in the state, and in the natural universe - levels that Shakespeare's contemporaries thought of as the microcosm, the body politic, and the macrocosm. It points out the necessity for the right exercise of power and the right governing of a commonwealth, as Prospero learns, even as he serves as a symbolic figure of the good man in his perpetual fight with evil.

IMAGERY AND SYMBOL

The Tempest, finally, is characterized by richness of **imagery** and symbol. It contains some of the greatest lines of English poetry, although it is not always possible to take them in isolation from the context of the play. They are functional in the action to a certain extent, as witness Prospero's great speeches. Or rather, they arise out of the dramatic situation at least slightly, and then go far beyond it, for nothing can really justify on dramatic grounds Prospero's great speeches in Act IV and Act V. It is the greatness of the sheer poetry of the play that has led to the feeling among many readers and critics that it is in its rich, strange, ambiguous world of illusion a work of almost limitless meaning and suggestiveness.

QUESTIONS AND ANSWERS

Some of the important questions that are often raised about the play and deserve closer treatment than we have been able to devote to them so far, may be stated in the following terms:

1. What does the character of Prospero signify?

2. How is Prospero related to his servants Ariel and Caliban?

3. May it be said that *The Tempest* is potentially another great Shakespearean tragedy? If so, how does it differ from tragedy?

4. What is the function of the Alonso - Sebastian - Antonio plot? Likewise, what is the function of the Caliban - Trinculo - Stephano plot?

5. How does Shakespeare obtain in his readers or the audience of *The Tempest* "that willing suspension of disbelief for the moment that constitutes poetic faith"?

6. What hard evidence is there that the play really contains allegorical elements?

7. What is meant by the statement that *The Tempest*, alone among the plays of Shakespeare, strictly observes the dramatic unities?

8. What are the elements of fertility ritual or marriage celebration in the play?

9. How is suspense maintained in the play, even though it is implied that there can be no suspense because Prospero is in control of everything at all times?

10. How is the problem of evil resolved in the play; is evil destroyed in the struggle on the Island?

11. May it be said that all on the enchanted island are in some way educated - and given deeper insights into reality - during the course of the action of *The Tempest*?

12. Is the conclusion of the play properly motivated and intellectually satisfying?

1. What does the character of Prospero signify?

While it is advisable not to consider Prospero simply an allegorical character, the fact remains that he seems to embody certain ideas and concepts of Renaissance society. He must be thought of primarily as a ruler; a ruler who embodies the primary virtues that Shakespeare's audience would have expected of a ruler: magnanimity, the ability to elicit obedience and to control the behavior of his subjects based on his superior intellectual, rational, and moral powers. Prospero's white magic, or theurgy, may have commanded belief from at least a part of Shakespeare's audience, but the magical powers have a symbolic value assigned to them; they represent Prospero's ability to master his environment and all other beings on his enchanted island.

Prospero may also signify Shakespeare's belief in the great potentialities of man: potentialities for good as well as for evil. Prospero, by mastering his lower passions for revenge on his enemies, proves, in the Elizabethan view, man's ability to control his own actions by an effort of will. He represents at least the possibility of free will. Even when Prospero is a stern ruler, as in his dealings with Caliban and with his own evil brother, Antonio, he is never a tyrant; he metes out justice, while inclining on the side of mercy.

2. How is Prospero related to his servants Ariel and Caliban?

If it is accepted that Prospero represents the highest intellectual faculty of man, Ariel may represent what Plato, in the Republic, referred to as the spirited faculty - the executive arm of the intellect - which must always be controlled by the intellect. Similarly, Caliban may represent the animal passions of man, which also must be under the control of reason and the intellect.

Both Ariel and Caliban need constantly to be restrained by Prospero, and in each case he fits the kind of restraint needed to the particular character with whom he is dealing, as Prospero generally does on the enchanted island. Thus he threatens Caliban when the man - monster is rebellious toward him; he also threatens Ariel, but in a milder way, when Ariel seeks his freedom before his time is out and before the work begun in the tempest is accomplished. About all that can be said here is that Elizabethan moral philosophy, based ultimately on classical thought, envisioned the human soul as having three levels: sensible, rational, and intellectual, or perhaps these may be called the animal or acquisitive soul, the spirited or executive soul, and the over - riding superior part of the soul, the Reason. Whatever the three levels are called, it was always clear to Shakespeare's contemporaries that the highest level must at all times be in control; this highest level is probably represented allegorically by Prospero, with the other two occupying roles subordinate to his by a sort of unchanging law of nature.

3. May it be said that *The Tempest* is potentially another great Shakespearean tragedy? If so, how does it differ from tragedy?

The answer to the first question is yes. At the beginning of the play, there is a potential tragic situation, especially as Antonio, a villain cast in the mold of an Iago or a Lady Macbeth, formulates his plot against the life of Alonso, King of Naples. We are convinced by Antonio himself that he is quite capable of executing his plot, and awaits only a favorable opportunity for doing so.

That opportunity does not come, because Prospero is already in control through his magic arts and his supernatural servants of everything and everybody on the enchanted island. No harm can come to anyone but by Prospero's permission, and after an apparent brief struggle with himself Prospero resolves that the "rarer action is in virtue than in vengeance." Thus he forbears to take the revenge on Antonio and Sebastian that he might well have taken, leading to a tragedy of revenge.

The action of the play, then, is resolved quite early. Evil is disarmed unknown to itself, whereas in the great Shakespearean tragedies, evil destroys itself and burns itself out in an action which cleanses the very moral order of the universe - but this happens at the end of the tragedy, and destroys good as well as evil. In *The Tempest*, the good are safeguarded from harm, and thus the tragedy remains only potential; it cannot become actual.

4. What is the function of the Alonso - Sebastian - Antonio plot? Likewise, what is the function of the Caliban - Trinculo - Stephano plot?

At the level of the dramatic, both plots heighten suspense in what would else be a rather static situation, since Prospero is so much in control of what happens on the island. Suspense is aroused as the audience wonders whether the attempt on the life of Alonso, or that on the life of Prospero, can be successful. Of course it cannot be, but Shakespeare underplays Prospero's supreme powers at first, so that we wonder if he does have complete control.

Further, the two plots, which balance off each other on the serious and the comic levels respectively, illustrate the educative action of *The Tempest*. The six characters involved learn what their moral duty is, despite themselves; they are all changed for the better, with the possible exception of Prospero's brother, Antonio, who is most clearly the major villain of the play.

Finally, at the level of allegory, both sets of characters may represent man's imperfect nature undergoing the discipline through the enforced initiation into the deeper realities of existence by Prospero's magic.

5. How does Shakespeare obtain in the readers or the audience of *The Tempest* "that willing suspension of disbelief which constitutes poetic faith"?

The primary answer to this question involves the frame of the "real world" that Shakespeare establishes at the beginning of the play. We are led away from the beginning situation - which occurs in the midst of reality: a storm at sea, with mariners fighting desperately for their lives - by more or less imperceptible gradations, until we come to accept Prospero's magic as a "natural" thing. By the end of Act I, Shakespeare has completed the dramatic **exposition** of the conditions on the enchanted island so perfectly that we are prepared to accept any marvels as everyday occurrences.

At the end of the play, Shakespeare must bring his audience back to reality, and he does so primarily by the device of Prospero's abjuration of his magic and his resumption of his duties in the "real" world of Milan. In between, it is the fantasy world that Shakespeare makes real, causing the audience, in Coleridge's famous phrase, to suspend its disbelief.

6. What hard evidence is there that the play really contains allegorical elements?

The evidence primarily comes from external sources; from recent scholarship concerning the way Shakespeare's age viewed reality, and especially from the moral philosophy professed by most thinking men in the Elizabethan age. Man's soul was generally thought of as multi - leveled, having sensible, rational, and intellectual faculties. This idea is not completely without credence even in our age; Freud's tripartite division of man's psyche into id, ego, and superego may form an analogy to this idea. In terms of their dramatic functions as well as their utterances in the play, it is hard not to believe that Prospero, Ariel, and Caliban must in some way form an allegorical representation of the three aspects of man's nature, whatever the terms used to describe these levels. Many of the speeches, especially of Prospero, are not motivated dramatically as they might be, and therefore it is hard to escape the conclusion that they have allegorical or symbolic content. The danger in interpreting *The Tempest* lies in the temptation to assign meanings too rigidly and too specifically to Prospero, Ariel, and Caliban.

7. What is meant by the statement that *The Tempest*, alone among the plays of Shakespeare, strictly observes the dramatic unities?

The three unities were found in the classical drama especially of the Greeks and of certain later periods, and were those of time, place, and action. In most of his plays Shakespeare was not disposed to observe them at all. The unity of time was a concept that specified that in a play all of the action should be confined as closely as possible to the circuit of a single sun. Extreme purists insisted that the play could last no longer chronologically than the exact time of the action on the stage, to maintain the illusion of reality. *The Tempest* apparently covers no more than four hours, and Shakespeare makes constant reference, through Prospero and Ariel, to the passage of time so that he makes the unity of time conspicuous.

As to the unity of place, everything takes place on a supposedly deserted island, except the storm in Act I, Scene I, and even that takes place so close to the island that it qualifies. The unity of place is thus exceptionally well observed in the play. The unity of action specifies that there should be no irrelevancies in the play and that all digressions and subplots should be avoided. Shakespeare has something of a subplot in the persons of Stephano, Trinculo, and possibly Caliban, but at the same time these are all tied together by the plot against the master of the enchanted island, Prospero.

It may be that in view of the fantastic plot and action of the play, Shakespeare observed the unities in order to obtain an increase in the verisimilitude of its effect, and further lead the audience to suspend disbelief.

8. What are the elements of fertility ritual or marriage celebration in the play?

Primarily these relate to the masque scene celebrating the betrothal of Ferdinand and Miranda in Act IV, and the affirmation of the proposed marriage in Act V. This is an important thread of the meaning of the play, for the marriage signalizes a return to the reality of the outer world; it is basically hopeful for we have been convinced that Ferdinand and Miranda are fit rulers to succeed to the thrones of Naples and Milan. It is hoped by all among the principals of the play that the marriage will prove fruitful; this was especially important in the case of a royal house, because if there were no heirs the line and the succession to the power would soon pass into other hands by default.

9. How is suspense maintained in the play, even though it is implied that there can be no suspense because Prospero is in control of everything at all times?

This is a difficult problem for the dramatist. Shakespeare resolves it by keeping many of the strands of Prospero's control out of sight - they are present by implication. He uses the slightly clumsy device of having Prospero "forget" the plot of Caliban against his life, and he allows the plot of Antonio and Sebastian to come near to threatening the life of Alonso. By the time we realize the full power of Prospero, we know that no harm can come to anyone on the island without his consent and knowledge, but by then the play is near its conclusion. In other words, Shakespeare reveals Prospero's full power gradually, thus leading to an additional element of suspense.

10. How is the problem of evil resolved in the play; is evil destroyed in the struggle on the Island?

The problem of evil is not resolved in the play, probably it could never be, even in that enchanted realm. What happens is that evil is pushed to the edge of reality, and it is overcome by the actions of those who are good.

There are several different kinds of evil in this play, and they are generally manifested by specific people. We have political evil in the characters of Alonso (to the least degree), Sebastian (who does not succeed), and Antonio, who has actually committed the ultimate political sin of usurpation, and as far as he knows, has also committed murder. The next kind of evil is the evil of the flesh, and that is manifested by Stephano and Trinculo, as the evil of drink, and also of greed. They are readily turned aside from an even greater evil, that of murder, by the sight of rich clothes hanging on a clothes line. Caliban also manifests this kind of evil in his reported attempt to rape Miranda. But by the end of the play he will "sue for grace."

By the end of the play all these characters are punished for the evil they have committed, or have intended to commit. Alonso thinks he has lost his son, Antonio fears vengeance from his forgiving brother. But these intellectual and political crimes are punished more than those of the flesh. Caliban will be wracked with agues, and the drunken courtiers have their ardent spirits dampened by immersion in a horsepond. Their desires are thus soon quenched.

11. May it be said that all on the enchanted Island are in some way educated - and given deeper insights into reality - during the course of the action of *The Tempest*?

Yes indeed! The Island possesses the educational value of an academy devoted to the study of morals, and in particular to the study of good and evil. At the beginning of the play the characters are set very clearly before us in terms of their respective attitudes to virtue. The moral states of the visitors to the Island, for instance, are shown to us through their individual vision of the landscape in Act II, Scene 1. Adrian, the neutral, notes the freshness of the air of the Island, while Sebastian and Antonio claim that it is full of foul smells. Similarly, Gonzalo, the man of virtue who saved Prospero and Miranda, notes "How lush and lusty the grass looks! how green!" Sebastian and Antonio, by contrast, see only parched land. In short, the Island is obviously enchanted, because each man sees it according to the amount of personal virtue he possesses.

Gradually, in the course of the play, the nature of good and evil is shown to us, and those who have done wrong are punished for their faults. Alonso, whose evil action was to aid Antonio in his usurpation of the dukedom of Milan, is in turn plotted against by his brother, Sebastian, and also the usurper, Antonio. He awakens from his dream to the literal reality of armed men standing over him.

In the same way, Gonzalo is again reawakened to the existence of evil in the world, and by the apparent death of Ferdinand, he sees the punishment that is inflicted upon Alonso. The King of Naples himself sees this for himself, and the more Gonzalo speaks of the advantageous marriage that the King had made for his daughter, Claribel, the more the King reproaches himself for having sent his daughter far away. This match has obviously been one for money and position, and for his ambition, Alonso believes himself bereft of his son as well.

Ferdinand and Miranda also learn. They discover the nature of love, virtuous love. At the same time, Miranda's knowledge of evil is reinforced, and the test of Ferdinand is not merely one of his constancy in love, but a test of his virtue as well. Both young people are shown in the process of physical and emotional maturing.

Caliban, the creature of the earth, learns too. When he says at the end of the play that he will sue for grace, he is showing that he has discovered that fine clothes are not in themselves a guarantee of a gentleman, or of virtue. He has learned to look beneath the appearance and can appreciate Prospero as his master now that he has seen the two courtiers, Stephano and Trinculo. These two characters have probably also learned, and they are punished through their flesh. Their punishment of being led through a horsepond is one that is fitting to their bestial natures. In effect, they are punished more than anyone else in the play, probably because Shakespeare saw them as worse than the others, because they have willingly permitted themselves to give in to the desires of their flesh and have become as animals.

Prospero himself learns, and he is taught by Ariel, the creature of the air. Initially it appears that Prospero had planned to take vengeance on his enemies, but Ariel notes that even he would feel pity for the court party, if he were human. At this implied rebuke, Prospero - whose abilities and knowledge are greater in effect than Ariel's, because he possesses a soul - swallows his wrath and forgives his enemies.

12. Is the conclusion of the play properly motivated and intellectually satisfying?

It certainly is, if one views it against the background of Elizabethan political and philosophical thought. While it may appear to be a great comedown for Prospero to resume his governing of Milan after having exercised supreme power on his island, still this is a socially superior role for him; a role in which he had originally failed, as witness his usurpation by his wicked brother, Antonio. Prospero voluntarily assumes the burdens of office again. Life must continue, in the real world: this is symbolized by the marriage of Ferdinand and Miranda, and the prospect of the union and continuance of the royal lines of Naples and Milan. The play, then, has a cyclical quality; it returns to a bright reality at the end, for the level of illusion symbolized by the enchanted island can never be maintained.

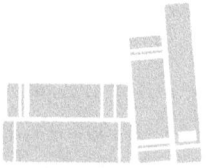

BIBLIOGRAPHY

The following list of books, grouped under several headings, may be useful if it is kept in mind that it is suggestive rather than exhaustive. Some of the works have been discussed in greater detail in the text of this study. The critical and interpretive studies are in no way presented as all equally sound and sensible. Thus, the books by Professor Tillyard and Professor Theodore Spencer are essentially accurate, suggestive, and useful on the backgrounds and possible meanings of *The Tempest*. On the other hand, the studies of the play by Colin Still and Emma Brockway Wagner, for example, are in general open to criticism, mainly on the ground that the evidence presented in support of their interpretations leaves something to be desired. It has been thought advisable to include some of the more extreme interpretations simply to show the great range and variation of possible approaches to the play.

SHAKESPEARE BIOGRAPHY

Bentley, G. E. *Shakespeare: A Biographical Handbook.* New Haven: Yale University Press, 1961

Chambers, E. K. *William Shakespeare: A Study of Facts and Problems*. Oxford: Clarendon Press, 1930. 2 vols.

Chute, Marchette. *Shakespeare of London*. New York: E. P. Dutton, 1949.

Halliday, F. E. *The Life of Shakespeare*. London: Duckworth, 1961.

Parrott, Thomas Marc. *William Shakespeare: A Handbook*. Rev. ed. New York: Scribner's, 1955.

THE THEATRE

Adams, John Cranford, *The Globe Playhouse*. Cambridge [Mass.]: Harvard University Press, 1942.

Baldwin, T. W. *The Organization and Personnel of the Shakespearean Company*. Princeton, N.J.: Princeton University Press, 1927.

Bentley, G. E. "Shakespeare and the Blackfriars Theatre." *Shakespeare Survey*, I (1948), 38-50.

Harbage, Alfred. *Shakespeare and the Rival Traditions*. New York: Macmillan, 1952.

Harbage, Alfred. *Shakespeare's Audience*. New York: Columbia University Press, 1941.

Nagler, A. M. *Shakespeare's Stage*. New Haven: Yale University Press, 1958.

SOURCES AND BACKGROUND

Cawley, Robert Ralston. "Shakespeare's Use of the Voyagers." *PMLA*, XLI (1926), 688-726.

Cawley, Robert Ralston. *The Voyagers and Elizabethan Drama*. Boston: D. C. Heath, 1938.

Craig, Hardin. *The Enchanted Glass*. London: Basil Blackwell, 1960. (1936.)

Curry, Walter Clyde. *Shakespeare's Philosophical Patterns*. 2nd ed. Baton Rouge, La.: Louisiana State University Press, 1951.

Gayley, Charles Mills. *Shakespeare and the Founders of Liberty in America*. New York: Macmillan, 1917.

Kermode, Frank, ed. *The Tempest*, in the "Arden Edition of the Works of William Shakespeare." Cambridge [Mass.]: Harvard University Press, 1958.

Lee, Sidney. "The American Indian in Elizabethan England." *Scribner's*, XLII (1907), 313-330.

Lee, Sidney. "Caliban's Visits to England." *Cornhill Magazine*, N.S., XXXIV (1913), 333-345.

Lovejoy, A. O. *Essays in the History of Ideas*. New York: G. Braziller, 1955. [Has an essay on Caliban.]

Lovejoy, A. O. *The Great Chain of Being*. Cambridge [Mass.]: Harvard University Press, 1936.

Lucy, Margaret. *Shakespeare and the Supernatural*. Liverpool: William Jaggard, 1908.

Marx, Leo. "Shakespeare's American Fable." *Massachusetts Review*, II (1962), 40-71.

Newell, W. W. "The Source of Shakespeare's *Tempest.*" *Journal of American Folklore*, XVI (1913), 234-257.

Nosworthy, J. M. "The Narrative Sources of *The Tempest.*" *Review of English Studies*, XXIV (1948), 281-284.

Reed, Robert R., Jr. "The Probable Origin of Ariel." *Shakespeare Quarterly*, XI (1960), 61-65.

Spencer, Theodore. *Shakespeare and the Nature of Man*. New York: Macmillan, 1958.

Tillyard, E. M. W. *The Elizabethan World Picture*. London: Chatto and Windus, 1943.

Ward, A. W. "Shakespeare and the Makers of Virginia." British *Academy Annual Shakespeare Lecture*, 1919. In *Proceeds of the British Academy* for 1918-19.

Welsford, Enid. *The Court Masque*. Cambridge [Eng.]: Cambridge University Press, 1927.

West, Robert H. *The Invisible World: A Study of Pneumatology in Elizabethan Drama*. Athens, Ga.: University of Georgia Press, 1939.

CRITICISM, TEXTUAL AND INTERPRETIVE

Bowling, Lawrence E. "The **Theme** of Natural Order in *The Tempest.*" *College English*, XII (1951), 203-209.

Chambers, E. K. "The Integrity of *The Tempest.*" *Review of English Studies*, I (1925). 129-150.

Chambers, E. K. *Shakespeare: A Survey*. London: Macmillan, 1926.

Clemen, Wolfgang H. *The Development of Shakespeare's **Imagery***. Cambridge [Mass.]: Harvard University Press, 1951.

Coleridge, Samuel Taylor. *Coleridge's Shakespearean Criticism*, ed. Thomas Middleton Raysor. Cambridge [Mass.]: Harvard University Press, 1930.

Collins, John Churton. *Studies in Shakespeare*. New York: E. P. Dutton, 1904. [Has article on the sources of *The Tempest*.]

Gesner, Carol. "*The Tempest* as Pastoral Romance." *Shakespeare Quarterly*, V (1959), 531-539.

Gilbert, A. H. "*The Tempest*: Parallelism in Characters and Situations." *Journal of English and Germanic Philology*, XIV (1915), 63-74.

Greg, Walter Wilson. *The Editorial Problem in Shakespeare: A Survey of the Foundations of the Text*. Oxford: Clarendon Press, 1942.

Hankins, John E. "Caliban the Bestial Man." *PMLA*, LXII (1947), 793-801.

Hart, J. A., Jr. "*The Tempest*." In *Carnegie Institute of Technology*, Pittsburgh, Department of English. Shakespeare: Lectures on Five Plays. Pittsburgh, 1958.

Kermode, Frank. *William Shakespeare, the Final Plays: Pericles, Cymbeline, The Winter's Tale, The Tempest, The Two Noble Kinsmen*. London: Longmans, Green & Co. for the British Council, 1961. "Writers and Their Work, No. 155."

Knight, G. Wilson. *The Crown of Life*. London: Oxford University Press, Geoffrey Cumberlege, 1947.

Knight, G. Wilson. *The Shakespearean Tempest*. London: Humphrey Milford for the Oxford University Press, 1932.

Major, John M. "Comus and *The Tempest*." *Shakespeare Quarterly*, X (1959), 177-183.

Muir, Kenneth. *Last Periods of Shakespeare, Racine, and Ibsen*. Detroit: Wayne State University Press, 1961.

Murry, John Middleton. *Shakespeare*. London: Jonathan Cape, 1936.

Ralli, Augustus. *A History of Shakespearean Criticism*. London: Humphrey Milford for the Oxford University Press, 1932. 2 vols.

Rose, Brian W. "*The Tempest*: A Reconsideration of Its Meaning." *English Studies in Africa*, I (1958), 205-216.

Schucking, Levin L. *Character Problems in Shakespeare's Plays*. London: G. Harrap, 1922.

Sisson, C. J. "The Magic of Prospero." *Shakespeare Survey*, XI (1958), 70-77.

Smith, Irwin. "Ariel as Ceres." *Shakespeare Quarterly*, IX (1958), 430-432.

Spurgeon, Caroline. *Shakespeare's **Imagery** and What It Tells Us*. Cambridge [Eng.]: Cambridge University Press, 1935.

Still, Colin. *Shakespeare's Mystery Play*. London: Cecil Palmer, 1921.

Taylor, George C. "Shakespeare's Use of the Idea of the Beast in Man." *Studies in Philology*. XLII (1943), 530-543.

Tillyard, E. M. W. *Shakespeare's Last Plays*. London: Chatto and Windus, 1938.

Traversi, Derek A. *Shakespeare: The Last Phase*. New York: Harcourt, Brace, 1955.

Traversi, Derek A. "The Tempest." *Scrutiny*, XV (1949), 127-157.

Van Doren, Mark. *Shakespeare*. New York: Henry Holt, 1939.

Wagner, Emma Brockway. *Shakespeare's The Tempest: An Allegorical Interpretation*. Yellow Springs, Ohio: Antioch Press, 1933.

Wilson, Harold S. "Action and Symbol in *Measure for Measure* and *The Tempest*." *Shakespeare Quarterly*, IV (1953), 375-384.

www.ingramcontent.com/pod-product-compliance
Lightning Source LLC
LaVergne TN
LVHW011712060526
838200LV00051B/2881